Richard Walters has written many books on human and business success but is perhaps best known as the inventor and writer of the Complete Advisory Solution, which is now used by thousands of businesses and individuals in Canada, the USA, Ireland and the United Kingdom. Richard lists his main loves in life as his family, football, travel, business and writing. He is married with three children and lives in Hampshire, England.

To Dad,
Here is something to
give you a good laugh

Rich W

AREN'T WE A FUNNY LOT?

Travels Around the British Psyche

Richard Walters

Book Guild Publishing

Sussex, England

First published in Great Britain in 2011 by
The Book Guild Ltd
Pavilion View
19 New Road
Brighton, BN1 1UF

Illustrations by Mike and Sheila Bastin Art & Design

Typesetting in Garamond by
Norman Tilley Graphics Ltd, Northampton

Printed in Great Britain by
CPI Antony Rowe

A catalogue record for this book is available from
The British Library.

ISBN 978 1 84624 566 4

Contents

Acknowledgements

My first acknowledgement goes to the World Wide Web, which provides every one of us with a rich resource of highly accessible information and without which I dread to think how else I could have researched the subjects covered in this book – perhaps by reading books! I am a great fan of the BBC News Website and the government is now very helpful in providing a large amount of official data through the National Statistics Office.

In this book I have attempted to refer specifically to all the sources of public data and reports, although of course I am unable to provide a comprehensive summary of each but acknowledgements to everyone nonetheless.

First, a big thank-you to my parents for, (a) deciding they were up to the challenges of child-rearing and (b) for providing a stable and loving environment in which to be brought up. For my part I wholeheartedly apologise for my teenage years!

Thank you to my wife, Marion, who has willingly given up many weekends, holidays and most evenings while I sat in our study researching and writing this book, plus I acknowledge her significant feminine feedback in ensuring balance at all times. My children's encouragement to continue writing once the first draft of Chapter 1 was in place was invaluable. A particular thank-you to my schoolteacher son, Tristan, for his very helpful initial feedback and editing, red pen and all: 'You could do better, Walters!'

Finally, I would like to say how much I appreciate Westminster City Council for their key part in inspiring me to actually write this book and beat my St George's Dragon. This must be worth celebrating and getting the flags out, but more on this later!

1

To Begin

Isn't Britain a crazy place in which to live? We are supposedly a civilised, tolerant, mature and affluent society and yet at the same time we manage to be illogical, continue antiquated rituals and sometimes verge on the completely off-the-wall. You may have found that life is far from perfect and doesn't always develop just as you planned, but you have to admit it's certainly interesting. We human beings do the strangest and most bizarre things, and this is what provides so much of life's interest, so let's explore the concept in this book that life in Britain is far too serious to take seriously.

It was one of the human race's best, the genius Einstein, who said, 'The definition of insanity is doing the same thing over and over again and expecting a different result.' In this book don't expect thought-provoking psychological insights into what drives people to do what they do, or the answers to any of life's mysteries or more important questions. Rather, we go on a journey through life's funny and surprising sides, starting with the weather, and including the joy of Christmas, the excitement of holidays, sleeping like a log, the frustrations of driving, the mad world of sex and ending, of course, with a smile.

You will notice that Einstein's quotation on insanity has been taken over by the personal development people and they would do well to take note that he also said, 'Only two things are infinite, the universe and human stupidity, and I'm not sure about the former'; he was a bright man that Einstein!

If E does equal MC^2 then it is possible you are reading these first paragraphs in a parallel universe, although statistically (more on this later) you are most likely to have purchased this book in one of this universe's friendly bookstores. Perhaps you might have borrowed it from a friend or you might be browsing the book in a comfortable modern store, possibly *before* you buy it, the book that is, not the shop.

Nowadays bookstores are very pleasant places to visit with soft sofas to lounge across and fresh coffee on tap, so don't worry if you think the shop assistant is checking you out because you're lurking;

please relax, sit down and read on. Did you know that more than half of books that are purchased are not completely read or even read at all? Amazing, isn't it? To find out, that is, that you're not the only one who has unread books all over the house! I keep mine under our bed, which I plan to use to soften the fall, just in case the bed collapses. I hope we can make this book one of the 50 per cent that is indeed red (curses on that spell-check) and I also hope you really enjoy it.

As life is too serious to take seriously, the only alternative is to laugh at it! Thank goodness we don't have to look too hard to find the bizarre or ridiculous, as it's there in everyday modern life. Being British provides us with a natural ability to engage with the most wonderful of our national and cultural traits and that is our willingness to laugh at ourselves. When it comes to self-effacing or self-deprecating, it's definitely better to Buy British.

For some time I have felt the desire to write a book, similar to this one, although the final push across the creative threshold came when I took a taxi ride from Waterloo Station and enjoyed the company of a London cabby. Do you agree that London taxi drivers don't necessarily fit the clichéd profile of that chirpy and witty Cockney?

I have found there are three types of London taxi driver. The first group of black cab drivers is made of what might be called 'Hermit Pimps'. These are taxi drivers who clearly would prefer it if you weren't in their taxi at all and appear to take great pleasure in letting you know this. They do this in less-than-subtle ways: by never looking at you, by using short, sharp sentences which are a series of staccato words and not really sentences at all, by adding a gruff or irritated tonality to their voice and in fact a whole demeanour that says, 'If you weren't paying me money I wouldn't give you the time of day. Now get out of my cab!' One has to say that they communicate all this very well indeed.

The second group of black cab drivers comprises what might be called the 'Angry Men'. These are taxi drivers who appear to have an inner frustration with life and your entry into their cab provides them with the perfect opportunity to vent this frustration and they do so with great effectiveness. You will be offered all their wisdom on a myriad of life's problems or, more likely, imagined difficulties. Before you know it you are involved in a conversation about the sort of right-wing politics you imagine break-away groups of the BNP discussing at covert meetings in the backroom of smoky East End pubs. Frankly, I feel very uneasy when they take the conversation down this path, although of course, being British, it's me that's embarrassed, not them.

This type of taxi driver seems to love the fact that you have entered their world and appears not to want the journey to end, as presumably the opportunity to convert you would then cease. The journey usually finishes with them saying 'Cheerio' in the certain knowledge they have found a fellow believer. The cunning look in their eye as you leave their cab says, 'See you at the next meeting!'

The third kind of black cab driver is made up of what might be called 'Real Deals'. This group is witty, amusing, friendly, intelligent, well versed in worldly matters, sensitive to your needs, articulate and a joy to meet. These people are the type of taxi driver that has created the chirpy Cockney profile. By the time your journey is over you might notice that you have told them a number of details about yourself that are certainly not the type of personal information you would normally disclose to a stranger you have only just met.

The payback is that you normally receive a kind comment or compliment such as, 'Blimey, you're fifty-five; I would never have believed it. Tell me then, what's your secret?' These types of journey often end with a mutual feeling of melancholy, just because this jolly experience is over. We wish each other well, in a similar manner to those holiday friendships with couples you meet in Crete, with whom you promise to stay in touch but never do so. I often walk along the pavement after such encounters thinking, 'You know life's pretty good. There are some really nice people on this earth', and in my opinion, that's an excellent thing.

During my inspirational cab journey from Waterloo Station, my taxi driver was a Real Deals type and it was because of this that what he said caught my attention. He told me that Westminster City Council had considered issuing an edict to all of London's licensed black cab drivers informing them that they were banned from displaying the flag of St George, particularly during the forthcoming St George's Day. He went on to compare this to the St Patrick's Day parade in Central London which would significantly disrupt traffic and he correctly concluded that the tricoloured flags were allowed on St Patrick's Day because this particular day brought in large amounts of tourist money.

It occurred to me how bizarre this apparent ban was and how far this action, which was clearly motivated by political correctness, had missed the point. It was the fact that my driver was apparently such a good type that I listened to what he said, because if decent and sensible people like him were frustrated, then this type of action had to be worth writing about. Now you can see why my first thank-you to all those who have helped me in the writing of this book went to Westminster City Council.

You have probably heard the phrase, 'Life is a journey, not a destination', and, thanks to my Real Deals cabby and of course Westminster City Council, this book is 'a journey, not a festering idea'. In fact, it's a journey across a number of interesting stops that highlights just how crazy life can be. Our journey with this book moves on through visits to a selection of life's more amusing aspects, to eventually finish, as all things should, with a big smile on your face (Happy Smiley People).

We will start, as does virtually every conversation in Britain, with the weather.

2

Awful Day Today

We begin with the weather or, to be more accurate, what we British people talk about when we don't know what else to say. It may be a complete fallacy to believe that only British people start conversations about the weather although, as a true Brit, I do seem strangely drawn to that odd behaviour of avidly reflecting with others upon the seemingly boring topic of the environmental effects of meteorological influences across the British Isles.

To be fair to us British, other factors are at play in these apparently compulsive openings to our conversations because as human beings our physical environment is very important to us and that's completely understandable. It offers reference points in our lives and provides us with some order – if it's hot it's summer, and if it's cold it's winter, though if only it was this simple.

Another possible explanation for our apparent fascination with meteorology is that it might just be laziness to start a conversation with the weather, because at least this guarantees some common ground. What happens if both people live in Antarctica? Their conversation would go something like this: 'Morning, cold today, isn't it?' – 'Yes.' Alternatively, how about people living in Death Valley? 'Morning, hot today, isn't it?' – 'Yes.' At least in Death Valley they could go on to say, 'Be cold tonight though, won't it?' The problem with living in places that have such minimal climatic variations is that you would actually have to start a conversation by saying something meaningful – help!

Another reason why we British talk so much about the weather is because our climate is temperate and, let's face it, boring. We don't really get any extremes of weather and yet we exaggerate conditions just to prove the place we call home is a 'living-on-the edge' type of territory. Listen to us talk and you would imagine Britain has the most interesting and wild climate in the world. Whatever do foreigners think when we start our climatic tirade? Of course the real reason we do this is because it's what we have been brought up to do, and, one has to admit, it's what we do very well indeed.

We have two inches of snowfall and the whole country grinds to a halt. Buses and trains are cancelled and people don't make it into work. We make those phone calls to our place of work in which we sound like Scott of the Antarctic with that well-practised hangdog, at-the-edge-of-human-endurance, explorer-type voice: 'I tried to get in, but I just couldn't make it.' When you call into work like this, don't you just feel like a naughty schoolboy or schoolgirl? That desperate and frail voice really takes some practising.

When it does actually snow, why do men get so focused upon how many inches have fallen? You never hear women talking about the estimated depth of a fall of frozen precipitation; it is only men. Men will argue about it and in great detail as well. 'Amazing, John, we've had four inches this morning.' 'No, I think we have had at least six inches. It was up to my patio!' When you see this in black-and-white, doesn't it sound like machismo? Still, if in doubt, it's always six inches, isn't it?

If we get a spell of slightly cold winter weather, all you hear British people say to each other are things such as, 'It's a nightmare! Terrible weather, isn't it awful?' No, no, no! Terrible weather is a tornado, a hurricane or a snowstorm that covers your car and a nightmare is when your roof is blown off.

Even the government wholeheartedly joins in with this well-practised over-reaction. They encourage us by issuing stern and grim warnings to the public: 'Unless your journey is absolutely necessary you are advised to stay at home.' It sounds like the sort of warning they might give us if there was a nuclear strike due in five minutes, not two inches of snow having just fallen.

We have a bit of warm summer weather with the sun out for a few days and straight away, yes you have guessed correctly, it's a heatwave. At the time of writing the highest-ever recorded temperature in Britain was on 10 August 2003 in Faversham, Kent at 39.5 °C (100 °F), which I admit is a bit warm. Consider this: the city of Palm Springs in California has three months each year where nearly every day of the month is *above* 40 °C (100 °F), so that's virtually 90 continuous days over 40 °C! Memorably one BBC headline on 11 August 2003 read: 'Tube keeps running in heatwave.' For heaven's sake, much of the London Underground is below ground and the clue is in its title. I wonder what the residents of Palm Springs would make of all this.

Whenever we have slightly abnormal weather, the news people roll out the now-familiar phrase 'Since records began...' This sounds very grand in a historically momentous way and clearly the type of thing you would never dream of questioning. I have looked into what this actually means and rather than the 'since the beginning of time' implication, 'since records began' means precisely 'since 1914'. This is surprising, isn't it, as I would have thought that this grand phrase would at least have meant since the mid-1800s? As a result, and to be accurate, we have records for 96 years. Bear in mind that human beings are generally considered by scientists to have been on Earth for approximately 300,000 years and for all of these years there has been 'weather'. Therefore, we only have records for 0.031 per cent of our time on the planet, which is not really a very extensive sample.

The reality is that we do have some records that extend back for a meaningful period, as the England and Wales Precipitation Series (rain) started in 1766 and the Central England Temperature Series (hot and cold) started in 1659. It seems these series are never used and I'm sure there are many valid scientific reasons why not. My hunch is that the real reason we don't use this data is because 'Yesterday was the 13th hottest day since 1659' just isn't a great media headline. What do you think?

The whole business of meteorological records is fascinating – honestly. What do you think is the driest month of the year in London? Unless you are a meteorologist or get this lucky 12-to-1 shot right, you are unlikely to be correct. The driest month is at the height of our good old, conventionally perceived as wet and cold winter. The driest month is surprisingly February, with an average monthly rainfall of only 1.34 inches.

The old adage that says, 'There is no such thing as the wrong weather, just the wrong clothes', is very true. However, despite this you see young people out on the streets on a cold January night dressed only in skimpy tops or T-shirts. Why do they do this? Is it because there is a current fashion trend to be a Designer Hypothermiac? For nine of the twelve months in a year, London's average monthly temperature exceeds 10 °C (50 °F) and, contrary to conventional wisdom and the opinion of virtually every US and Australian citizen, there doesn't seem much evidence to support the theory that the UK is a cold place.

I find this surprising and encouraging, but there is another piece of data that is less reassuring. If you are left stranded in, not *on*, the English Channel at the height of summer, your 'Time Dependant Survival Probability' is that of only having a 50-per-cent chance of lasting 12 hours. In February it's just a matter of a couple of hours. Interestingly, and very reassuring for a big man like me, if you have an extra 5 millimetres of fat on your body you might last up to a further 8 hours. I must admit to adding an extra couple of slices of bacon to my breakfast this morning just in case we do ever go down over the Channel.

In Melbourne, Australia, December is the middle of their summer season. Conventional wisdom in Britain says that Australia is a hot sunny land and we Brits have visions of sandy tropical beaches and warm seas lapping yellow shores. In fact, the average sea temperature off Melbourne in December, at the height of the Australian summer, is only 16 °C (60 °F) whereas at Bournemouth in August it's 18 °C (64 °F). Two degrees is not much of a win for the English, but we don't get many wins over the Aussies, so let's savour this one. Of course if we take them on in Brisbane we get thrashed by a full cricket team of 11 degrees – F!

Let's focus now upon that frustration of all frustrations to those of us living in Britain and especially southern England, which is, of course, the hosepipe ban. We live in a land that, because of its position in the Gulf Stream, is generally moist and, let's be fair, well watered! This is why everywhere is so green and even when it's not

11

quite so green we need to acknowledge that this hardly constitutes a drought. Surely, all we need to do is draw on the water reserves our water-keeping officials have so carefully stored away for us in the times of abundance? Apparently we can't and for some unknown reason the powers-that-be tell us we will certainly run out of water at some time – well, possibly, by chance and if conditions don't change (which they will).

Probably the reason we can't use our hosepipes in the summer is due to the fact that we often get the wrong *kind* of rain, which I assume is that type of rain that doesn't include much water. I leave you with this telling thought on the subject of hosepipe bans. The resolute residents of Palm Springs, who live only 316 miles from Death Valley, the hottest place on planet Earth, generally have deep-green lush lawns surrounding their houses and they probably don't even know what a hosepipe ban is!

The day following the hottest day ever in Britain, this was reported by the BBC: 'The heatwave has brought with it violent thunderstorms, heavy rain and lightning.' Doesn't this just confirm two things we all know about the British weather? Firstly, we get a couple of days of warm weather and, before you know it, we have a thunderstorm and it's all over. Secondly, we exaggerate our weather – as we never just have thunderstorms, we have *violent* thunderstorms. Truly violent thunderstorms are the type you get in Florida or Malaysia, where the storm scares you half to death, the earth vibrates with a deafening sound and arrowed bolts of electricity light the sky, not a couple of claps of thunder and a bit of rain.

I have experienced only one hurricane in my life and this was while on a family holiday in Charlotte, Florida. They say you never forget your first time with a woman and they are right. This lady's name was Allison. The storm developed on 2 June 1995 and dissipated only on 6 June 1995 and therefore her life was remarkably, but not sadly, short. We had rented a condo right on the beach on the west coast of Florida. The storm was just hitting when we checked in and I can still recall my brother-in-law running ten yards from our car to the office to collect our keys and coming back looking like he had jumped into the swimming pool fully clothed. The winds were incredibly fierce and the clouds rolling in seemed to merge with the sea and strangely they looked just like fog ... that is, until the 'fog' reached you and gave you a major jolt to your senses.

It was a frightening and amazing experience and luckily the storm skirted us by. Imagine my surprise when I undertook some research on Hurricane Allison and found that she was only a Category 1 hurricane. Whatever would it be like to be at the centre of a Category 4 hurricane? Despite her Category 1 rating, Allison still managed tragically to kill one person and cause $1.7 million worth of damage, which is not bad for a first-grade lady!

Do you remember the 1987 hurricane in southern England? If you lived through this, it was a horrible experience and I feel very sorry for anyone who suffered its effects. However, by definition this wasn't actually a hurricane, which was why it didn't get a name! The maximum gust was recorded at Garleston, Norfolk, at 121 miles per hour at 4.24 a.m., which is a bit windy. Michael Fish MBE, the BBC weatherman, is much-quoted as saying on 15 October 1987: 'Earlier on today, apparently a lady rang the BBC and said she heard there was a hurricane on the way. Well, don't worry, if you're watching, it isn't.' Interestingly, Michael has subsequently said he wasn't actually talking about the weather in the UK; he was responding to someone who was worried about the weather in Florida just prior to a family member flying there on holiday, where there were fears of a Caribbean hurricane going Florida's way. He did actually say, 'Batten down the hatches', and that it would be 'Very windy across the south of England'. Not a lot of people know that but, still, it gave Michael his eternal place in history.

Have you noticed how in Britain, whatever the conditions, we are never happy with the weather? When it's hot and sunny you hear people moaning about how they can't sleep at night, and when it's frosty you hear people complaining how bitter it is. Irony of all ironies, when it's somewhere in between, that is mild and moist with a bit of sun, all you hear people saying is, 'I wish we had proper seasons like we used to.' They are actually wishing for extremes, probably in order that they can have a good old moan. Possibly this is the attraction, wanting to control the absolutely uncontrollable and then having something to *really* complain about.

We have four seasons and, just in case you have forgotten, they are: winter, spring, summer and autumn. I'm suggesting we look at the year as more than just a number of climatic seasons, but as something akin to our real-life human experiences. With this fresh perspective the year goes more like this; starting with December and in this month, in case you forget what time of year it is, Noddy Holder shouts from every department store's speaker system to remind you that 'It's Christmas!' Without doubt the festive season, together with its emotional fallout, deserves its own chapter and it rightfully has one later in this book.

After Christmas we move into the 'Black Winter Hole' and psychologists have actually highlighted the third Monday of January as the darkest day of the year, and they mean emotionally dark not the day of least sunlight. Apparently, it's due to the festive season post-traumatic let-down experience, plus the fallout from having overeaten and drunk too much alcohol. It is also around this time that we all receive our credit card statements showing our Christmas spending, the weather is dismal and it is physically very dark as well. I wouldn't be surprised if, like me, you feel depressed just reading about this dark time.

Survive these two months and Easter follows along, which means bunnies, spring lambs bouncing around the fields (you can almost smell the mint sauce), wearing a jumper not an overcoat, and more daylight hours. It's a wonderful time of optimism and hope. Then we are into those long days of May and June where it isn't dark until late and all manner of outdoor activities are possible for a full 18 hours each day, beginning at 4 a.m. right through until 10 p.m. – that is, if you have the stamina.

Next up, it's July and August and the delicious height of summer, the holidays and all those childhood memories of both languid hot summer's days and rain beating down on the caravan roof. There is still time in September and October for a bit of an Indian summer before the next black month of November. This time of year means plenty of storms, breaking your back picking leaves off your lawn, mending broken fences and the start of the nights drawing in. There it is, the year from a human perspective. Oh dear, it seems that's another year passed.

We now have a medically recognised condition that doctors call Seasonal Affective Disorder, or SAD. Apparently women aged 18 to 30 are most at risk. The symptoms are quoted as sleep problems, overeating (remember this could be handy if you are downed in the Channel), anxiety, guilt, despair, family and social problems, loss of libido (not enough snow), lethargy, stomach problems and joint pains, to name just a few. I would like to know how you identify when you have caught SAD, as most of these symptoms could easily be called life!

It seems that approximately 2 per cent of the people in Northern Europe suffer from this disorder and if you are one of these people you have my sympathy. Bright light affects the brain cells and our production of melatonin serotonin. So it seems when it's not sunny the melatonin just keeps right on going. It has been suggested that standing in front of a bright light of 2,500 lux for 30 minutes a day sorts the melatonin out. I'm not sure if this is true, as it might just have been put into the media by the Norwegian Electricity Board to enhance winter energy sales.

I decided to research some facts on the happiest and most miserable countries on Earth and to see if SAD was a factor. I felt the two statistics that would be the most helpful were the World Health Organisation's statistics on suicide rates and alcohol consumption per capita as I have a vision of a sad Norwegian man, sitting all on his own in a hut beside a fjord. It's pitch dark outside; he has an empty whisky bottle beside him and is contemplating ending it all.

15

Surprisingly, SAD favourite Norway is placed 39th in the list of highest suicide rates and 81st for alcohol consumption, so sadly that's another blow to our British self-congratulatory conventional wisdom.

Let's look at how we really do then: in the UK we have the 66th highest suicide rate and the 18th highest alcohol consumption. You often hear people in Britain state a desire to go and live in France and then go on to praise its easy-going way of life. Before you run off to the La Rochelle estate agents and look into buying your *gîte*, I would suggest you ponder this: France has the world's seventh highest intake of alcohol and the 20th highest suicide rate. Of course all this proves is that you can't trust statistics, as *on average* nine out of ten quoted statistics are inaccurate. Just remember: if you had your head in a hot oven and your feet in a freezer, you would, on average, be enjoying a perfect temperature.

One superb and completely life-affirming World Health Organisation statistic is that four of the five countries in the world with the lowest suicide rates are based in the Caribbean, which is, at least, encouraging. You see, it's true: 'Don't wur-ree, man ... be 'appy.' Pass me a rum punch – glorious!

We couldn't finish a chapter on the weather without mentioning global warming. This is a truly complex issue that seems to elicit fierce emotions. On Wikipedia, the free online encyclopaedia, at the time of writing there were a full 21 pages on the subject. In fact, the references, most of which are complex scientific papers, reports or books, total an amazing 127 documents! The Kyoto Protocol on Climate Change was completed in 1997 and the Treaty expires in 2012. At the time of writing the Treaty covered 160 countries and only two countries in the world had not yet ratified it and global warming was open again for yet more discussion in Copenhagen in December 2009. As you know, this talking has led to an agreement to talk some more!

The two countries that did not sign the Kyoto Protocol were Kazakhstan and, significantly, the United States of America. Al

Gore has won an Oscar for his film *An Inconvenient Truth*, a movie that very effectively puts the case for acknowledging that global warming exists. Before everyone in Britain gets excited about a year-long BBQ season, it's worth remembering that, if Al is correct, Brighton, Bristol, Manchester, Newcastle and large parts of London will be under the sea, which means the Cotswolds could get fairly crowded and Homebase in Cirencester is bound to run out of charcoal.

Despite Al Gore's sterling efforts, the people of the USA seem less concerned about global warming than the rest of us, although the citizens of Kazakhstan seem to be taking their non-participation in the Treaty much more to heart than the Americans, confirmed by their ranking of seventh in the world suicide league table!

I won't win any prizes in Kazakhstan now, but 'Que sera sera, whatever will be, will be (we're going to Wem-be-lea)', which brings us suitably to the next subject: sports and hobbies.

3

It's Only a Game!

The weather can ruin many a sporting event but it can't destroy a good game of Scrabble. Modern sport is typically driven by money matters and the media has created many a sporting celebrity. I doubt if many wealthy celebrities participate in Scrabble, although there are a number who are well known for their love of a particular sport, examples being Elton John and Watford FC and the Oasis boys and Manchester City.

It is probably a fair assumption that celebrities wouldn't have the necessary patience for a hobby. This implies that famous people are very often skin-deep and have more important things in their life than the need for a hobby. Initially this seems particularly judgemental but perhaps it's not completely unreasonable, as, however hard I try, I can't imagine Paris Hilton snuggled up in her luxury pad, sitting with a friend enjoying a nice game of dominoes.

The assumption might be that celebrities' lives are full of excess: fine wine, beautiful women, toy boys, five-star hotels, gambling, drugs and champagne and that's all in just one day. They probably don't have time to fit in even the smallest amount of trainspotting. However, if by chance you do see Posh Spice, armed with a clipboard on Clapham Station's Platform 4, then we are clearly not seeing the bigger picture and we all stand corrected.

Of course most famous people don't play sport but watch it. We partake of hobbies, we play games and we watch sport. The *Oxford English Pocket Dictionary* defines a hobby as, 'An activity done regularly in one's leisure time for pleasure.' The editor couldn't have got stuck on a difficult jigsaw then, because in these circumstances it doesn't feel like pleasure, more like pain. I have a theory that people have only one real hobby. We may sometimes desert our hobby for a period of grace, we may flirt with other hobbies, but we always intend to return! For instance you often hear people say something similar to, 'When I retire I'm going to get back to painting.' This reflects the difference between a hobby and a pastime, as a hobby, just like a dog, is for life; and a pastime, just like a cat, passes in and out of your life in phases, when it suits itself!

Maintaining this theme of analogies, there is possibly some parallel between a hobby and a pastime, and a spouse and a lover, although I suspect if one was to refer to one's wife or husband as a hobby, one would be in full receipt of all the strife one deserved! It's true that hobbies and spouses both fill your time and you certainly don't have time for more than one; practice makes perfect, both can be extremely frustrating and once you have made the complete model it often ends up on a shelf and gets dusty.

Despite this, there is clearly no excuse for inactivity in our country because there are so many hobbies to choose from. Consider these extensive choices: collecting items such as postcards, bottle tops, badges, cigarette cards, fridge magnets, rock music memorabilia, doll's houses, teapots or stamps; or hobbies such as bridge, marquetry, radio-controlled boats, hot-air ballooning, mah-jongg, battle re-enactment, origami and, of course, dominoes. With so many varied and obscure choices there really is no excuse to be bored. Incidentally, marquetry is 'The craft of covering a structural carcass with pieces of veneer forming decorative patterns, designs or pictures', but, of course, you knew that, didn't you?

Just imagine, in the privacy of your own home, or in quiet parts of the countryside, you are able to: play with model cars, buy and sell classic magazines, pretend to kill people, dress up as a Nazi, collect direct-marketing materials, have a book full of carriage receipts from around the world and in my case, with regard to hot-air ballooning, scare yourself half to death! I found one collection hobby that I have to admit had the least attraction of all. Amazingly, there is a club where people get together and talk about their common passion for Burger Toys. Well, it's a free country!

My personal sporting love is football or, if you are in North America, soccer. I have heard it said that you are hooked on the team you support from the day you first go along to a game. In my case it was when my dad took me, as a ten-year-old, to see Southampton (the Saints) versus Rotherham, for an evening game on 25 November 1964, which amazingly we won 6–1. Just like heroin or cocaine – and for the record, I have never tried any non-prescription drugs – you're hooked: a few wild highs but generally speaking, a series of dark lows and a continuous intense yearning. Both habits cost a large amount of money to fund, can break up marriages and both defy all logic. How many times have I asked myself, 'Why do I do this?' Funnily enough I never actually answer my question, just shrug and think to myself, 'Next time maybe.'

Supporting a football club takes many forms, though we will start by excluding football hooligans as these people are clearly not supporters in the true sense. For the rest of this chapter when we refer to supporters, let's agree we mean law-abiding and tax-paying citizens. Of course not all fans are the same. For example the 'OCD Fanatics' are the group who follow their team to every corner of the country. It is hard to argue with the suggestion that there is a degree of obsession displayed by this group. To wake at 5 a.m. and drive 400 miles, stand in the rain, get soundly beaten, drive back to arrive home at 11 p.m. and all this at a cost of probably in excess of £150, one has to say, appears somewhat compulsive. Paying £150 to be physically discomforted, beaten and emotionally let down is an interesting choice, although I have heard there is a leather-clad lady in Bromley who would do this to you for under £80!

Another group of supporters are the 'Steady Eddies' and these are the group who, as regular as clockwork, turn up to most home games and go to important away games, except, of course, on their wedding anniversary, when they quite properly miss the match. We also have the 'Good-Timers' who support their team but go to games only when times are good and either the team is playing well or the match is a big game. As in life, you can't depend upon this bunch.

Worse still are the 'All Talk' group who say they support a team but don't know any of the current team other than the stars and have a very loose allegiance to the club. This support is more akin to 'Keeping up with the Jones': they just want a designer team so they can be like everyone else. These All Talk supporters usually support a top Premiership team and frequently live hundreds of miles away from the ground and rarely, if ever, see their team. OCD Fanatics and Steady Eddies intensely dislike the All Talk types. The Steady Eddie group have deep respect for OCD Fanatics. Good Timers are mistaken by All Talks as Steady Eddies and, needless to say, All Talks don't have a clue what an OCD Fanatic is all about.

If you support Manchester United the experience of supporting your team would be very different from my experience of supporting Southampton. There would certainly be less dark lows and many, many, more wins. However, and here is the perverse nature of life, when Manchester United win a trophy it can't be as extraordinarily exciting, uplifting, emotional or sublime as for those supporters of, for instance, Coventry City enjoying a once-in-a-lifetime experience when they beat Tottenham Hotspur to win the FA Cup in 1987. It becomes boring when you win all the time, or so I'm told and, in my case, a chance would be a fine thing.

They say you can change your wife but not your team and as far as I'm concerned this is just plain sexist insensitive nonsense, although in the wives/football team game I'm 2–1 up, which is indeed food for thought. I originally thought my wife hated sport generally but as the last 20 years have passed I have realised this is not true. I have managed to get her to attend a number of sporting events, often by bribing her with good food and fine wine; rugby internationals, rugby league, motor racing, basketball, baseball (four times), ice hockey, American football and soccer. When I reflect upon this, it is interesting to note that at every one of these events she has added to my overall enjoyment of the experience, with one notable exception – football – where she is, without doubt, a pain-in-the-backside.

I once asked her why football was the exception and she told me it was because she feels frustrated by the exaggeration of football's importance and place in life. She feels there is little escape from it as the whole family and colleagues at work like it and the media is full of it. No wonder she feels like a Solzhenitsyn-type dissident, trapped in this over-egged football culture. Bill Shankly famously said, 'Some people think football is a matter of life and death. I assure you, it's much more serious than that!' Perhaps this is the type of thing my wife and others like her object to, and they might just have a point.

What football does offer is an alternative topic of conversation to the weather and this must be a good thing. At a business meeting I attend regularly every month we normally commence by discussing the status of our three football teams. It's very comforting for us and I dread to think how well the rest of the meeting would develop without this common and familiar ground. Like it or not, in the British Isles, football is a key part of our culture; it is more than a game but you can see why it is felt to be boorish for those outside the box and there is no penalty in that.

The game I played after my initial youthful football career was golf. Golf ought to be part of every standard therapy programme as the game encapsulates many of life's classic emotional difficulties. One could also suggest that therapy should be provided as a standard part of the golf club subscription! It has been said that golf is a 'good walk ruined' and there is little doubt that the social life that surrounds golf is a major attraction.

My golfing career (have ever words been more misused), like many other golfers', started with the usual catching of the golfing bug with the 5.30 a.m. early-morning starts to avoid the excruciating embarrassment of being watched when standing on the first tee, swinging your club and taking two feet of soil and turf that carefully shift the ball 6 inches. Such a lot of physical effort, mental concentration and emotional input for such a small return! Sounds like me in the bedroom and I'm not sure which is the more embarrassing.

The next phase of your golfing career usually involves joining a recognised club and learning the extensive rules and regulations regarding etiquette. When you sign up to a golf club they let you know the enormity of being committed to the rules, regulations, dress code and course etiquette. Golf committees take all these rules very seriously and becoming a member of a golf club is similar to signing up to the Official Secrets Act.

Golf is a great excuse for men to do many things that would otherwise be difficult to justify; for instance, flying off with a group of other married men to sunny climes without your wife and at great cost, drinking too much alcohol, staying up late, shaking hands a lot, gambling, frolicking in the sand, hugging each other and riding around together in little buggies – magic!

The sad end to my golfing career came when I caught both of its deadliest diseases, the 'yips' and then the 'shanks'. For non-golfing readers I should explain that a yip is the state you get into when faced with a short 3-feet putt. You suddenly have a dry mouth, your body shakes with fear, your wrist freezes to the side of your body and you have to literally force yourself to move your hands to the golf ball to get any form of forward momentum. Not unsurprisingly, you always miss the hole.

A shank sounds as disgusting as it actually feels! The worse thing about a shank is that every muscle in your body indicates to your brain that the ball is going in one direction and in fact it goes in the opposite direction – at right angles! This is utterly disconcerting as it defies everything you feel and is completely demoralising. The yips and shanks are to golf what erectile dysfunction is to the bedroom, except there is no golfing equivalent of Viagra; and so I gave up the game for good!

Fishing is a sport I have always felt I would enjoy and it is much quoted as being the most participative sport in the UK. Therefore it must have plenty going for it. The fresh air, the camaraderie, the relaxation and great big doses of quiet time are supposedly great attractions. To be precise, these major benefits seem to appeal more to men than to women, as the various angling clubs and specialist websites covering fishing seem to have virtually no female contributors. Why is this? Can it be that all this quiet time has less appeal to the fairer sex?

In fact, fishing is in many ways a metaphor for the battle of the sexes, as fishermen (the clue is in the title) seem to have a strange relationship with their fish, in that they have a passionate interest, a deep yearning and compulsion to catch that ultimate fish. It takes the form of a zoological intensity and yet fishermen also take great delight in stalking, tricking, teasing, yanking, dragging and of course weighing their prey. I can't imagine why this would all sound and feel so familiar.

Fishing is a notable absentee from the extensive list of sports included in the Olympic Games. Why is this – surely it would make great TV? The first Olympic Games are generally considered to have started in 776 BC when Koroebus was the first Olympic running champion. The Roman emperor Theodusius outlawed the games in AD 393 in an attempt to reassert Christianity. This intervention by religion and politics is a continuing trend in sport and in fact sport was effectively banned in England in 1642 by the Long Parliament and not restarted again until 1660 when cricket, boxing and horseracing were reinstated at Winchester and Eton colleges, which does tend to indicate that sport back then was not a common pastime of the peasants.

The modern Olympic Games started again in 1895 and were funded by the Greek philanthropist Evangelis Zappas and if ever a human being had an appropriate name, it is he. How many people would have the evangelical drive to recommence something that would zap us for over a century?

The Olympic Games have been regularly disrupted, or have almost been disrupted, by politics and the result has been tragedy, violence, drugs and boycotts. Today the Olympic Games are clearly too good an opportunity to make money to ever think of cancelling them! The Summer Games every four years have had 18 host countries with no individual country having hosted the Games any more than on four occasions. There are some notable countries missing from the list of previous hosts and every four years the population of these countries must feel like sporting pariahs. These Cinderella sporting nations include Spain, New Zealand, South Africa, Ireland and Argentina. These are proud countries that have enriched the world's sporting history and it's not fair. Give them a break and give them the Games. Let them lose loads of money on them, not us!

Perhaps we can look forward to a major improvement in our railway system as a result of the London Olympics 2012, or possibly not, which brings us suitably to the next subject: rail travel.

4

The Railway Children

In this country it is considered good sport to hammer the train operators but in the spirit of Lionel Jeffries and Jenny Agutter (if you know who they are, you're showing your age), we won't criticise them … well not much.

There is a group of people who probably know as much about trains as any other group and these people are known as commuters. Therefore, my initial research on this subject was a conversation with my brother-in-law who is a recovering commuter and who now works from home to escape the torturous commute to London. His emotive response to my questioning was to say, 'Commuting, I'm only now recovering from 30 years of hurt.' He went on to tell me about his experiences when he was a regular commuter from leafy Hampshire to London Waterloo. On Sunday afternoons he started to feel a general nervousness and a strange hollow feeling in the pit of his stomach, his mouth steadily became dry and a general feeling of dread descended upon him. He is not one for excessive emotional outpourings and as our conversation on commuting developed I could hear in his voice the strength of emotional memories being dredged up. To emphasise this, his words said everything about the potential horrors of commuting: 'It's only now, some five years later, that I can bear to get on to a train without feeling that dread.'

How is it that an inanimate object of 350 tons of metal, wood, plastic, little mock lights, fancy electronic displays and fabric can generate such deep emotions? It may appear somewhat inaccurate to describe a 350-ton object that moves at 110 miles an hour as inanimate. However, strictly speaking, it *is* inanimate, as it cannot move by itself. A train needs human beings to move it and the *Oxford English Pocket Dictionary* definition of inanimate is, 'Adjective: Not alive, especially not in the manner of animals and humans; inanimate objects like stones; showing no sign of life; breathless.'

Let's see how we do with this definition of inanimate in relation to trains. 'Not alive' – both the locomotives and the commuters on Monday morning seem to readily match this description, with of course the notable exception of Thomas the Tank Engine who is very much alive and well. 'Showing no sign of life' – it's difficult to justify this definition, especially when a train scares you to death, as it hurtles past your platform, gently caressing the air around you. 'Breathless' – this is definitely a good match, especially when the air conditioning breaks down on a hot summer day.

In September 2003, *Which?* magazine found that 82 per cent of commuters suffered a late train at least once in the previous five days, although no doubt this has all changed now. It really doesn't matter what the definition of 'late' is; the important thing is that commuters felt their train arrived late at their destination. Given this, and using the government's statistics, then why did, on average, 1,086,402 people commute into Central London every day in 2001? Surely not just for the money?

To ensure fairness and balance on behalf of the train operators I would like to put to you an alternative perspective. Imagine if you were responsible for running a train from Bournemouth on the south coast to Manchester Piccadilly and you were charged with ensuring that at every one of the 18 stations en route, in this 4 hours 55 minutes' journey, you cannot be more than five minutes late at each stop. You have to be on time at Brockenhurst, Southampton Central, Southampton Airport, Winchester, Basingstoke, Reading, Oxford, Banbury, Leamington Spa, Coventry, Birmingham International, Birmingham New Street, Wolverhampton, Stafford, Stoke-on-Trent, Macclesfield, Stockport and Manchester Piccadilly. From this perspective the train operators' task appears much more challenging, especially with so many variables at play. Would you like this job?

Let's consider what these variables might be. It's quite clear that one of those expensive consultancy firms has got to the train operators and told them that they 'must effectively engage with travellers' needs, by regularly communicating to customers regarding delays'. In itself who can argue with this? Doesn't it all sound very reasonable and simply like good business practice? Let's look at some examples of this effective communication and the crazy reasons we are given for delays which are all so blandly and yet entertainingly articulated to us when we are waiting on a platform or better still when we actually get on the train.

Most of us are aware of the now famous excuse of 'the wrong type of snow on the lines'. However, there are other excuses and here are just a few personal experiences. On a train I was travelling in, the guard formally and sternly announced that the problem was due to 'a delay in leaving the departure station'. Now call me old-fashioned, but I fail to see how stating the totally obvious just because the system says you need to is in any way effective communication. Another example of this unintelligent approach to communication was when one guard apologised and proudly stated that the delay was due to 'unexpected events'. Surely not?

However, I must return to my brother-in-law for the best experience of all: 'We apologise for the delay, which is due to two cows on the line at Winchfield.' Bearing in mind the train had just smashed into both cows at 80 miles an hour, to the obvious physical and visual knowledge of all those on board, this seemed like over-the-top communication. If only there were consultants around who could advise on common sense.

It's no surprise that when travelling on trains this bizarre environment encourages us to behave in a particularly strange way. I'm an amateur at this commuting business and actually feel quite inadequate when rubbing shoulders with professional commuters. You can see them a mile away and their whole approach is a routine that has been fine-tuned over many years. On the one hand I am in awe of their carefully crafted techniques, but on the other hand I feel sorry for them, as they are clearly suffering from some form of mild compulsive behavioural disorder. It reminds me of the lions you see in wildlife parks who compulsively pace up and down their cages. Don't you feel much the same about commuters as you do about lions in a zoo, in awe of their talents but somehow knowing it's not right for animals to suffer like this?

There are a number of behaviours that give away the professional commuter. The first clue is when you see them standing on the platform waiting for the train. They know exactly where the door will stop and you have this incredible sight of a bunch of grown men and women huddled quietly together around an illusionary spot, desperately concentrating on not feeling foolish, with yards of space either side of them. Amazingly it works and the train door usually stops within a couple of feet of where the huddle is positioned. If I was a train driver, I would see this every day and change the place where I stop, just by a few yards each day. I would think of this as a form of aversion therapy for the passengers' obsessive compulsive disorder. As my actions would clearly be politically incorrect, perhaps it's a good thing I didn't achieve my childhood dream and become a train driver.

I must admit to full participation in the next odd behaviour. Imagine you are sitting in your seat, in a group of four seats either side of a table. The main objective is to defend your space and protect that seat next to you as fresh passengers get on to the train at subsequent stations down the line. The proven technique to defend a seat is to spread yourself out as wide as possible, put the seat rest up, extend your papers across the whole table and stare out the potential dangerous attacker as they approach.

Of course, for those brave enough, the practically fail-safe method, still not without its risks though, is to smile warmly at any interloper as they approach, with a slightly crazed expression on your face and lovingly tap the seat next to you. This technique is pretty much foolproof but, as you can imagine, if it goes wrong, it goes wrong in a major way, as you might just attract the co-traveller from hell.

Rail travel is generally speaking very safe, but please be aware of three dangers when travelling on trains. The number-one danger is mobile phones. Have you noticed that when a mobile phone rings everyone in the carriage goes to their phone as if the call is for them? Why do people speak so loudly into their mobile phones?

Their conversation is at least 20 decibels above normal conversation and here's the oddity: if people knew this, they clearly wouldn't talk so freely and yet they must be aware of this tendency, as all they have to do is listen to other passengers on the train shouting into *their* mobile phones.

Some time ago I was on a quiet middle-of-the-day train home and a passenger two seats in front of me started a clearly important business mobile phone conversation. The call was obviously a very confidential and private conversation and it was embarrassing to hear. I wanted to approach the man and warn him of his imprudent actions. Did I do this? Of course not. I listened to every word, as did the rest of the carriage, and that's the problem, because however hard you try, you have just got to listen, haven't you?

It's not just business conversations either. I was sat opposite a thirty-something professional woman who proceeded to call her husband, Alan (who, incidentally, 'had lamb chops in the oven that would ruin unless she was home soon'), and have what can only be described as a very personal conversation about a few of their 'longer-term marriage issues'. I have to admit I was squirming at the degree of intimacy of the conversation and no, it wasn't about their sex life – at least that would have been interesting – it was about the sort of mundane but highly personal things a husband and a wife regularly discuss, but for goodness' sake, in private!

After she completed her call, I had an overwhelming desire to talk to her and offer to help, as it felt as if together we had shared something quite intimate. I didn't and I'm sure if I had done this, she would have felt it very inappropriate behaviour on *my* part. Please can anyone explain to me why all decorum seems to vanish when people have a mobile phone in their hand?

The number-two danger when travelling on trains is sleep, which is a danger to you and a danger to fellow passengers. How alluring is it to see dribble slowly sliding down a stranger's cheeks or worse still to listen to their gentle snoring, interspersed by lion-like snorts? When they wake up there are always a number of passengers knowingly looking at them – oh the embarrassment! Professional commuters call this behaviour NDS, or Nodding Dog Syndrome.

My brother-in-law told me of an occasion when he fell asleep on the train and woke up with a jolt. Instinctively his legs jerked out and he inadvertently kicked a young woman opposite him on the shin, very hard. She started to cry gently with the shock and pain, which must be an appalling memory for both of them. I never asked him what he said to her – perhaps 'Sorry' or maybe 'Oops' or probably, worst of all, 'I have some ointment in my bag. Would you like me to rub it on?'

Sleeping on trains is quite understandable as often you have risen early and worked a long hard day and, just like a baby in a pram, it's the motion. Don't ever mix alcohol, trains and sleep, unless of course you want to travel to the end of the line, as no one will dare wake you up before you arrive at the last station on the line, which in my case is Exeter St David's, some 127 miles from home, or so I'm told!

The number-three danger on trains is to forget your glasses or, more specifically, not to wear your glasses when visiting one of those fancy new toilets. The problem is caused by all the high-tech one-touch buttons of Open, Close, Lock and Panic. The buttons are in a line and you will see many an old lady apparently in 'panic mode' when all she wanted to do was lock the door. Worse still is to be sitting on the toilet with your trousers around your ankles, realise you haven't locked the door, aim to press Lock, but inadvertently press Open.

Commuting seems to encourage us to become anti-social, competitive and rude, as well as bringing out the worst in us. I think nothing reflects this better than my brother-law's passing comment to me: 'I started off my commuting career by giving up my seat to old ladies. No one else did, which meant I never had a seat. Eventually I realised that, if I ever wanted a seat, I had to stop giving it up. So I did and I found I could keep my eyes down on my book, ignore everyone else and survive the commute.'

Before finishing with trains we have to reflect upon possibly the most off-the-wall train people – those people (again to achieve a sense of fairness and balance) who absolutely love trains. Of course these people are best described as trainspotters. There are approximately 100,000 trainspotters in the UK, which is 9.2 trainspotters allocated to each of the 10,902 locomotives featured in *Rail Enthusiast*. I think my last comment indicates that I don't really understand what trainspotting really entails. One of Al-Qaida's first major successes in harming our cosy Western lifestyle was to force a trainspotting ban on stations, for security reasons. Those cunning terrorists, hitting us where it hurts most!

I love train journeys, especially long trips if I can afford a first-class ticket. You can work, read, stretch your legs (not so hard as to make people cry of course), eat, drink and generally relax. In comparison to an airplane journey it wins all hands down. Except of course, when travelling on commuter routes, in rush hours and when the fares are prohibitive.

I recall a Virgin Trains trip I took from London Euston to Manchester Piccadilly. I paid for a single first-class ticket on one of those great online sites and the fare was only £28.20. The stewards and stewardesses all had nice red uniforms and looked exceptionally smart; we had papers, magazines, our own little table and then they brought hot food on a trolley, all dished up in those cute little compartmentalised trays, just like flying used to be like before low-cost airlines ruined everything. It was like having my own picnic and was just lovely and there is no better word to describe the experience properly.

I liked it so much, I confess I rather indulged myself with the free red wine and when I arrived in my Manchester hotel I prudently decided it would be much better for me if I waited a couple of hours before I called my wife. I did wait the prescribed period and she was none the wiser. All this for £28.20 – lovely!

I wonder if traffic wardens travel by trains very much. I doubt it, as they probably prefer giving tickets to buying them. They don't know what they are missing with all that free red wine, which brings us suitably to the next subject: careers and jobs.

5

It's More Than My Job's Worth, Mate

When I was a young boy I actually wanted to be a train driver – and who put that bizarre thought into my head? I am assuming it was Casey Jones who was 'a-steaming an' a-rolling', although like many other of my more extravagant boyhood ambitions, this one sadly didn't reach fruition. However, my excuse for this relatively modest career ambition is that when I was a child there were still steam trains on the lines and thus some element of glamour remained about rail travel.

A pre-recessionary survey in 2007 showed rail transport operatives as being paid an annual salary of approximately £30,000. This doesn't appear an insignificant salary, certainly compared to other jobs featured in the same survey, such as paramedics' £21,000 or travel agents' £15,000, so maybe Casey Jones had a point after all.

Have you noticed how nowadays every job title is cleansed to the point of confusion and the perverse result is that this seems to sanitise the role to the stage where it means nothing? What is wrong with train driver or conductor, both of which we all understand? These job titles have some backbone, some meaning, some history, some substance, even some glamour and I can't imagine how anyone could consider them in any way derogatory. Instead of playing around with political correctness we may as well go the whole way and retitle these jobs to 'Inanimate Object Steering Operative' and 'Transportation Receipt Auditor'.

Strangely, I am quite attracted by this fancy new PC style of describing jobs and here are a few more sanitised job titles designed to make everyone feel more important: Junior Communication Media Distribution Officer – paperboy; Sanitation Operative – cleaner; Transparency Enhancement Engineer – window cleaner; Field Nourishment Facilitator – waitress; Domestic and Therapeutic Technician – housewife; Veneer Colour Technician – painter and decorator; and, to *finish* up (sponsored by), Excess Gastronomic Materials Hygiene Operative – dish washer.

Despite this excess of sanitisation, isn't there a strange attraction to this diarrheic way of describing a job? Rather than being a part-time writer, I like the idea of being an Intermittent Creative Literary Development Operative because it sounds much more complicated and thus surely more valuable. You no longer have an excellent Royal Mail postman who delivers your letters and just as importantly your direct marketing leaflets; you receive service from a top Monarch-Accredited Social Communication Distribution Officer. Property developers become Dwelling Entrepreneurs and, good news for my son: he ceases being a primary school teacher and becomes a Phase-One Human Knowledge Transferor! Doesn't work just become enriched by this new way of talking? ... Perhaps not.

My wife has told me a tale of her life many moons ago when she was a young unattached woman. Back then the technique she occasionally used to gently ward off unwanted attention from men at discos was to fabricate a career as a mortuary assistant whose job it was to regularly assist the coroner with post-mortems. She tells me this was a very successful and sensitive way to let men down, although I'm fairly certain the sensitive part is questionable.

Embalming itself is a sensitive subject and it must be an interesting and rewarding career, as embalmers deliver a very necessary service to families at a time when they really need help. There are approximately 1,300 qualified embalmers in the UK belonging mainly to the British Institute of Embalmers (BIE), which was founded in 1927. There is an obvious and quaint appropriateness in the title BIE, given that embalmers play a key part in helping friends and family say 'farewell' to their loved ones as they leave this mortal coil. I believe we should take our hats off to them for doing such important work in no doubt challenging conditions, because this is surely a job where you don't get to meet too many breathing people and conversation is, to say the least, limited.

In today's world we all receive plenty of training, often on the job, and with this in mind I would love to be at hairdresser school on the day they teach the new girls 'client conversation'. All the girls at my chosen salon are extremely friendly, helpful and good cutters. Unlike most clients I am happy to take pot luck with whichever stylist is free, as I normally book an appointment on a day coinciding with some free time. Incidentally, doesn't being called a client straight away make you feel grand and important? It's much better than being called a plain old 'customer'.

I should explain for the benefit of female readers that, unlike lady clients, who I'm sure truly get to know their stylist and exchange gifts at Christmas and on birthdays, we men keep an appropriate distance and therefore would do our best to refrain from using names and ensure the conversation is friendly but not too intimate.

Doesn't going to the hairdressers more than anything else highlight the differences between the sexes? Men treat going to hairdressers as a necessary, albeit enjoyable, chore; your hair grows, you get it cut. For ladies the visit to their hairdresser is part of an elaborate process of making themselves look as good as they possibly can. Because of this it is understandably elevated to a high level of importance in a woman's life; 'I like to make an effort with how I look.' Although men do now visit salons rather than the traditional sawdust-and-spittoon joints, they still treat the whole thing as a necessary chore.

My youngest daughter recently arranged a 'consultation' with her stylist to discuss the implications of her forthcoming hair appointment which involved changing styles. The consultation didn't involve any cutting, shaping, washing or dying, but rather it involved a form of 'hairdressing therapy'. I assume the consultation went something like this (for the sake of brevity, to maintain confidentiality and to protect the innocent I've left out the responses): 'How do you think you will feel once you have this new style?' – 'I see' – 'Did your mother ever have her hair styled this way?' – 'Interesting' – 'Do you feel you have any fear or pent-up anger about this?' – 'That's OK, this is quite normal' – and I'm sure much caring consideration was sensitively provided. Needless to say, it all went well: my daughter has no pent-up frustration and her hair looks great, so *vive la différence.*

Hairdressers' devotion to client conversation is admirable. On one particular visit to my salon I was lucky enough to be granted a stylist who had cut my hair many times before. She proceeded in the normal way by first asking me when I had last had it cut. I love the way they casually flick through your hair when they ask you this and at the same time peer into the mirror over your shoulder as they do so. I can never remember how long ago my last haircut was, so I make something up and this seems to please them as they always knowingly smile to my answer with the nod saying it all, 'You have left it too long ... again.'

Next up was the delightful washing of your hair. Is there a more relaxing experience than having your hair washed this way? The head massaging is exquisite and makes your toes tingle. It's even better than a good game of dominoes. We then move back into the chair to start the game of client conversation. You probably know the drill yourself: 'Do you work in town?' – 'What do you do?' – 'Are you on your lunch-break?' (even though it's 3 p.m.) – 'Have you had your holidays yet?'

We proceeded to run through the question-and-answer session, all in the right order, and I assumed she had just forgotten who I was, which was understandable and I took no offence at all. However, I was very wrong and, once we had dutifully completed the client conversation process, she proceeded to talk to me about my granddaughter. Hairdressing Training School must be an amazing cult-like place to gain such dedication to client conversation.

Do you remember *The Two Ronnies* sketch from a number of years ago where Ronnie Corbett answers Ronnie Barker's questions, but answers the question that Ronnie Barker asked previously? If I were to do this at my next haircut appointment the conversation would develop something like this: 'Do you work in town?' – 'No, Tenerife'; 'What do you do?' – 'I'm close to you here'; 'Are you on your lunch-break?' – 'It's quite difficult to explain, but I travel a lot'; 'Have you had your holidays yet?' – 'No, I will probably go to the sandwich shop up the road.' Having said this I love getting my hair cut, meeting some pleasant and friendly people and always leave the salon nicely refreshed and relaxed, so thank you, girls (and boys).

There are any number of unusual and less than appealing career paths that I'm glad I avoided, such as: chicken sexers (who examine baby chicks to determine if they are male or female in order that they can be separated to get them ready for a short lifetime in a shed 20 feet by 20 feet – no thanks!); celluloid trimmers (thank goodness this is not what you first thought – it is celluloid you trim not cellulite, by shaving the excess celluloid bands on golf clubs to ensure the leather grip stays in place); artificial inseminators (who insert bull's semen into a cow's organ, though at least with gloves on); and odour testers (who smell armpits to test for deodorant effectiveness – 'When's lunch?').

However, as far as I'm concerned there isn't any more unappealing job in Britain than that of Prime Minister. At first glance the job has real appeal: absolute power, nice London city-centre townhouse supplied as part of the job, big office just down the road and overlooking the river, nice car with a chauffeur, plenty of overseas travel and decent expense claims. On further consideration you find the real downside of the job: your contract is only for a maximum of five years, your middle managers (the Cabinet) all want your job, the minute you get the job everybody in the country thinks they can do your job better than you (especially taxi drivers), most CEOs get paid ten times what you do, while in the job you visibly age at an incredible rate (did you see what it did to Tony Blair?), and worst of all you get only four hours' sleep a night. Plenty of nice hotel rooms but no time for dominoes!

The modern world has brought us a new range of strange and bizarre careers that were not around when people had less leisure time and needed to spend all their hours working hard to pay the bills and keep a roof over their head. One such job is that of pet psychologist, which in a country where approximately 50 per cent of families own at least one pet has some market potential.

Twenty years ago I assume the country was inhabited by only a handful of airbrushers, but in today's world of physical perfection and elf-like models, a good airbrusher is essential. Whatever is it like spending every day of your working life from nine to five focusing in fine detail upon celebrities' moles, cellulite, pimples, needle marks, bloodshot eyes from a hard night's partying and, before you get your hands on them with your 'airbrusher', a layer of extra body fat?

The Office of National Statistics released a survey called the Annual Survey of Hours and Earnings and the 2007 pre-recession survey showed some interesting facts. The lowest-paid groups in the range of under £10,000 per annum included cleaners, hairdressers (they are not paid enough), fast-food restaurant staff, school cooks and swimming pool attendants. However, in this group are a couple of surprises: fine artists and holiday representatives and if ever two groups of people should stay well apart it's these two, as I suspect they would have little in common except the alcohol.

The highest-paid group earning between £100,000 and £500,000 a year include the obvious candidates of high court judges, entrepreneurs, Cabinet ministers, NHS chief executives and the Prime Minister. However, would you also expect to find in this group private psychotherapists and quarry managers? Surprising indeed, although at least it's comforting to know that a quarry manager can afford the necessary therapy fees to deal with his or hers explosive 'Dynamite Post-Traumatic Stress' symptoms. In total, the survey covered 221 different categories and there can be no doubt that when it comes to how to earn your way in life, there is more than one way to skin a cat and I'm guessing that, in certain Chinese takeaway restaurants, skinning cats is one of them!

Another interesting job must be hotel receptionist as so many people pass through your life with such interesting interactions: sordid affairs with secretaries, brawls at Irish wedding receptions, romantic weekends to re-energise marriages, couples rowing, drunken lecherous conference-goers, lonely overnight business travellers, celebrity rock star revellers, mystery shoppers from head office, hotel inspectors and many more. You have to endure this bedlam taking place all around you…and whatever is it like to be sitting at your reception desk at 12.30 a.m. and know the earth is moving, right above your head?

Much has changed over the last 40 years and not least is everyone's attitude to work. In the 1960s and 1970s no one expected to enjoy their job: it was a case of paying the bills and maybe having some money left over for a few little luxuries. Today everyone expects to be fulfilled and to have a job that will stretch, challenge and reward them. The old working-class approach of clocking in and clocking out on the exact hour has almost totally gone.

Today in our modern digital world the lines between work and home have blurred. Many people regularly stay late at work and in some companies there is a culture that says, 'If you leave before 6.30 p.m. you're not really committed.' Many people now 'hot-desk', which means sharing desks because employees are never permanently in the office and working from home is common. When we are at home we log into the office and reply to our emails, and when we are at work we chat with friends on Facebook, look at sports websites and similar, through a host of different forums or chatrooms. The digital revolution has certainly blown away the old working-class employment habits.

It seems that our time at work is now much less fun. The job might be considerably more interesting, but the human interactions are too earnest and possibly excessively technologically driven. When I was an 18-year-old fresh-faced trainee, although our job was extraordinarily boring, the human interaction was hilarious. I spent the first three months of my training contract clearing out the office cellar, shredding paper (those staples are a pain) and burning the results in our office's garden. No health-and-safety risk assessment then, no time-and-motion study and no 360-degree review of my fear of rats, but I did get a pair of overalls that nearly fitted me!

In times gone by there was far less focus upon efficiency,

probably because we only cost tuppence h'apenny to employ and we could while away whole afternoons becoming experts in games such as table cricket using a rolled-up piece of paper, a ruler and a matchbox as wickets; getting a paper ball in the bin after bouncing it off as many walls as possible; or shove ha'penny. Those were the days and such talent now lost.

My least favourite service people are those who use their role definition to actually avoid performing their job. I refer of course to 'jobsworths' – 'Sorry, mate, it's more than my job's worth.' These people avoid doing anything helpful at all and quite frankly doing the job they are actually paid to do. I was enjoying a relaxing few days in the Lake District with my wife and we caught a small ferry from one end of a lake to the other. Out of season these ferries run about every hour. We were on the ferry as it was casting off and a middle-aged man with his young son was running to catch the ferry. The ferry was no more than three or four inches away from the dockside when the man got to the gangplank. However, he was told in no uncertain terms by a member of the crew that he couldn't join the rest of us because 'The boat has left!' All it would have taken was to move back in and tie up for him to come aboard and our journey would have been delayed by no more than two minutes, but we didn't and I guess the ferry worker felt very powerful. Well, it's more than my job's worth to disclose which route this was and therefore I won't … Oh go on then: it was Ambleside to Bowness-on-Windermere!

Before we can achieve gainful employment, we often have to prepare and submit the dreaded curriculum vitae or CV. It's incredible how a couple of simple Latin words have lasted so long in regular use. It's very impressive as not many ancient words can boast this amount of longevity. I wouldn't be surprised if these are the only Latin words most people are familiar with and actually use in their day-to-day language. The Latin words *curriculum vitae* mean 'course of life', which is grand in the extreme, and if you have more than one CV (to suit the occasion of course) these are curricula. As you read this, students all around the country are preparing their CV including many exaggerations and expansive words to highlight their special attributes, such as: self-motivated, detail-oriented, ambitious, goal-driven, professional, well-organised, independent, flexible, and the inevitable team player. I wonder how many of these student fiction writers understand that they are summarising their 'course of life' to date; it's worth a thought.

During my working life my own least favourite job was when as a student I undertook one particular part-time summer job. The pay was excellent and the few weeks' work helped fund many months of liquid jolliment. The job was potato picking and quite frankly it was desperately difficult. You might wonder how picking up a few potatoes was difficult but this was back-breaking work, even for a young man. The tractor drove up and down the field bringing potatoes to the surface and our job was to pick them from the earth and place them into a basket. Unfortunately, by the time the tractor had returned to your spot, you had only just filled your last basket.

There was no break, other than to your spine, and by the end of the day your back was in tatters. Each day seemed to drag with boredom and the sheer physical exertion simply drained your will. I gained a tremendous insight into how prisoners must feel on the chain gang – you could say I was handed a cool Paul Newman experience without the hard-boiled eggs. It was during these weeks that I made a commitment that never left me and my mantra was to focus on my studies and work hard in order that I never, ever, had to go back to the fields again.

Without a shadow of a doubt being a Father Christmas beats potato picking but I wonder what those Father Christmas impersonators in department stores and garden centres do in January, which brings us suitably to the next subject: Christmas.

6

Have a Lovely Christmas

One of the best jobs at Christmas must be that of Father Christmas in a department store: children don't weigh much, you're nice and warm wrapped up in your comfortable outfit, no one can recognise you, your excess weight doesn't show and best of all you get to be nice to everyone. Think again, because it was estimated that the average number of children who visited each Santa Claus in American shopping malls over the festive season was 10,119. No doubt the invention of 'Repetitive Child Syndrome' and all its symptoms is just around the corner. Time to call in the 'no win/no fee' lawyers!

Christmas is such an emotive time of the year, with people having high expectations of the perfect family Christmas – fun, games, parties, presents, good food, fine wine, classic TV, relaxation and family bonding. Unfortunately for some, the reality is some-what different. The American Heart Association published a study in 2004 which showed that more Americans die of a heart attack on 25 December than any other day of the year. Worse still, the second most fatal day is Boxing Day and the third most dangerous day is New Year's Day. We're doomed, Captain Mannering, unless of course we Brits are very different from our transatlantic cousins.

Despite these statistics, Christmas can be a wonderful time of the year because we can be children again and generally let our hair down. Who doesn't feel that rush of anticipation when the Christmas tree first goes up? However cynical one might be, a Christmas tree, well decorated with all those colourful flashing lights, and presents cosily hugging the base, says, 'Home Sweet Home'. It is true that there is a degree of stress in ensuring all your presents are purchased and the list is fully crossed off, but there is a real joy in wrapping a loved one's present and craftily placing it at the back of the tree to stop them feeling the box.

My favourite part of the whole of the festive period is Christmas morning, particularly after the presents are opened and the food is on its way. There is bustle everywhere as the table is being laid, music plays softly in the background, everyone is happy, excited and the first drinks are being opened. 'Merry Christmas' said then has real meaning, and don't you just have a warm glow remembering Christmases past?

One notable exception to all this jolliment is the experience of putting up the Christmas tree lights. Whoever designed these gadgets should get the Nobel Prize for 'The Science of Testing Human Patience'. Christmas tree lights seem to be designed to the highest specification and as far as I can establish include the most incredible movement detection gadgets. Each year you pack them nicely away on 5 January and then place them in the loft for 344 days and nights, never approaching them once in this time. When they were put into the decorations box they were working perfectly and when you lay them around your tree some 344 days later – nothing! No timer could be that precise, because I have tried different days – 343, 345 and 346 – and yet every time you plug them in, not a bulb in sight is alight. Therefore, I have deduced they must include a hidden motion detector that is triggered when you bring them out of the decorations box, which in turn is linked to a device in the lights that then blows everything. It's a perfect invention to frustrate you and ensure that every single year you go out and buy two new sets of lights! Of course that's not before you have changed virtually every single bulb, screwing the little devils in tightly just in case. It's ingenious!

Unfortunately, this is often the first of Christmas's challenging frustrations. It is possible we set ourselves up for disappointment over Christmas, quite frankly because our expectations are too high and, for a lot of people, unrealistic. We have all understandably bought into the media fantasy Christmas represented by films such as *It's a Wonderful Life*, which incidentally, like many people, I love. As we grow from childhood to adulthood it is inevitable that our memories of Christmases past are those of our formative years, simple presents, family gatherings, extra freedom and no school. With an enhanced awareness of life generally and greater responsibility, it is hardly surprising that, as we grow up, a little of the gloss wanes.

The excellent news for us all is that when your children or grand-children are at that age you can start the magic all over again. It really is true: Christmas is for children, plus obviously Christians. BBC TV's *Newsround* programme found that 89 per cent of children were excited by the prospect of Christmas and this is wonderful to hear, isn't it? As far as we adults are concerned, it's probably a time to enjoy excess, drink, food and drink again, because during December alcohol consumption increases by 40 per cent.

Of course, Christmas is a Christian religious festival that com-memorates the birth and life of Jesus Christ. The theological think-tank Theos conducted a survey by ComRes and found that of 1,000 people surveyed only one in eight people could answer correctly four simple biblical questions about Christmas. It is not clear if the 25th of December is actually Jesus' date of birth as they didn't have Outlook then! It is thought the date may have been chosen to correspond with the winter solstice or perhaps a Roman festival. Christ's Nativity, based upon the Anno Domini system of dating, is thought to have occurred between 2 and 7 BC. This is surprising because you would have thought we could have been sure that Jesus' date of birth was 25 December AD 0.

A survey by the *Daily Mail* found that, of 5,500 cards in high-street stores, only 67 had pictures of a biblical event. As a society we now seem confused as to what Christmas really represents. Sabir Hussain Mirza, 2008 chairman of the Muslim Council of Oxford, speaking about the fact that council leaders in Oxford changed the title of 'Christmas Lights' to 'Winter Lights Festival', said, 'Chris-tians, Muslims and other religions all look forward to Christmas, I'm angry and very disappointed. Christmas is special and we shouldn't ignore it' – good man.

In fact 3 million people attended church over the two days of Christmas and Boxing Day, which beats the 2.7 million people who watched football, rugby and horse racing over the whole festive period ... and well done to anyone who on the same day went to church and also watched the Saints.

Because of the opportunity to have time off work, party, gather your family together, eat and drink too much and spend huge amounts of money, many other non-Christians have decided to join in the fun and who could blame them? Active Christians understandably resent this perceived hijacking of their religious festival by the media and non-Christians. Christmas, or that horrible phrase Xmas (incidentally, replacing 'Christ' with an 'X' appears disrespectful in the extreme), has become littered with ironies.

One particular irony is the well-known classic Christmas song 'I Believe in Father Christmas' by Greg Lake. If you listen to the lyrics, you will hear that the song is partly about Christmas being taken over by commercialisation and losing its meaning and yet, irony of all irony, what do you hear but a poor cover version of Greg Lake's great song every single year, on the hour, in every department store or retail outlet. He would never have expected or planned that his song, with its important message, would be used in this way to promote the very thing he objected to, though I bet he loves the royalties!

Another irony is that the festive season is seen as an important time to celebrate family values and strengthen bonds. Good idea, but according to the Family Mediation Helpline more than 1.8 million couples will have contemplated divorcing their partner during the Christmas period and Relate say they have a 50-per-cent surge in calls in January. In fact 8 January 2009 was the UK's busiest ever day for divorce lawyers. If you survived that day, then romance is alive and well!

Experts say the reasons for this might be due to couples spending too much time together, the effect of intense 'quality time' with relatives, financial pressures, excessive alcohol consumption and the idea that January is a time for big change. I'm convinced these apparent problems are due to one reason and one reason only and that is unrealistic expectations and thus inevitable disappointment.

However, this high-brow attitude is blown apart and taken back to crude reality by an InsideDivorce.com survey that found that some 36 per cent of men cited 'lack of sex' as their reason for divorce. My goodness, some things never change – men!

One of the headlines you may have missed prior to Christmas 2008 was: 'Taliban blow up Christmas turkeys destined for British troops'. A consignment of 325 kilograms of frozen turkey roll breasts, bound for Helmand Province, was destroyed in an explosion. Our 3,000 very brave troops did get a traditional Christmas and were duly fed and feasted upon replacement turkey and 148.8 kilograms of sprouts. I do have a safety concern about this, as surely the audible result of eating that many sprouts would give away the position of any scouting party to the enemy? This particularly callous attack by the Taliban compares unfavourably with the famous Christmas Day truces of 1914 and 1915 in the World War I trenches. In Ypres' no-man's-land, soldiers from both sides exchanged gifts, sang carols and played football even though the higher level of military command hated it.

Our brave soldiers on active duty deal with real danger every day, although there are other less significant dangers presented by Christmas back home. According to the Royal Society for the Prevention of Accidents (is the Royal Family particularly clumsy?), 'A typical Christmas Day is rife with danger.' I have to say I have from time to time been anxious about the festive season going well and worried whether we would all successfully socialise together, but I hadn't really ever seen Christmas Day as an actual minefield, rife with danger.

The Royal Society for the Prevention of Accidents predicts that each Christmas approximately 80,000 of us will go to hospital after festive accidents. Apparently the main danger areas are: cuts from knives (opening presents, not stabbing your spouse), falling off rocking horses, smashing new bikes into walls, falling over electric cables, nasty burns and gravy exploding in the microwave. One of the most dangerous items is the good old Christmas tree, which alone is likely to bring down 350 of us. My goodness, Christmas is a dangerous time.

If this were not enough, researchers from the group Consensus Action on Salt and Health, or CASH, found that a typical Christmas Day lunch contains twice the daily recommended amount of salt and if eaten every day would be dangerous. Forget the salt; if I ate a Christmas dinner every day I'm not sure what would get me first, bursting or liver damage, but both definitely before the salt. During a normal Christmas in the UK we consume 10 million turkeys, 25 million Christmas puddings, 250 million pints of beer and 35 million bottles of wine, so no wonder we are shattered in January. An amazing 7 million mince pies are left out for Santa on the fireplace and I now realise who keeps this myth going: it's the marketing people at Mr Kipling!

Christmas supper is a unique experience, isn't it? It feels like only a couple of hours since you feasted to bursting point and some bright spark says, 'Does anyone want supper?' Inevitably no one answers but that doesn't stop the host. Before you know it, the table is full of pork pies, cheese (ten varieties!), salad, Branston Pickle, pickled onions, a whole side of ham, cold meat left over from Christmas dinner, loaves of bread, crisps, sausages, Scotch eggs and, as if that weren't enough, a Christmas cake and a Yule log. I don't think we have ever actually got to eat a Yule log in the last 20 years, but still we buy them and roll them out every single year. The ritual of bringing out this Phase Two trough of food, leaving it out for a couple of hours and then putting all of it back in the fridge is really quite charming, isn't it, but you have to do it, don't you?

Bubble and squeak on Boxing Day is excellent and turkey curry the next day is tolerable, but by day four the leftovers look unattractive and in fact an estimated 120,000 of us get food poisoning at Christmas, although only 4,000 are reported. We seem to accept that a bad tummy at Christmas comes with the territory. The Food Standards Agency recommends eating leftovers within 48 hours, which is quite simply impossible.

As a boy my family Christmases were enriched by a pet dog called Kim. She was a lovely mild-mannered cairn terrier and certainly didn't deserve the Judas treatment that our family gave her on Christmas Day. Inevitably, a meal of sage-and-onion stuffing, dried peas and sprouts eventually takes it toll on the human digestive system, usually by late afternoon to early evening. A less than pleasant aroma would periodically pervade the lounge and one of us would say, 'Oh Kim, that's horrible!' We all knew it wasn't her, but of course this gave us all more leeway ourselves, poor dog.

When I was a child we weren't quite in the immediate post-war situation my mum remembers: 'Back then I was glad to get a satsuma as a present.' I remember my late uncle making me a wonderful cavalry fort which must have taken him months to build, and how many presents can you remember some 40 years later?

Nowadays my family helpfully give me their Christmas lists with the full description of the required item: which online store features the best deal, its recommended retail price, a link to their website and importantly the 12-digit order serial number! Everybody gets what they want and we all pretend to be surprised: 'That's just what I wanted! How did you know? Thank you, darling.' In a way it *is* a surprise, because it could easily have been 'temporarily out of stock'! Next year a hand-made cavalry fort for a 55-year-old man goes on my list.

The problem today is that we live in a pampered Western civilised world where, if we want something, we buy it and what's more instantly. What can you buy the man, woman or child who has everything? Unfortunately, the answer is often, 'Something to put in a cupboard and take to a car boot sale later in the year.' I can see a time in the future when the ideal gift will be a 'credit card payment gift voucher' and thus we would have a strange method of passing money around: I buy you a gift voucher in December, you use it to pay off your credit card in January, having yourself built your debt up by purchasing credit card gift vouchers for me in December. I truly believe in the old adage that says, 'It's the thought that counts', and if you believe this, then any gift from a loved one is truly wonderful, which is sentimental but well worth re-engaging with.

What about the cost of Christmas? It's getting out of hand, isn't it? We bought 27 million mince pies (not my family, the country), of which as we know about a quarter went stale overnight on the fireplace and were wasted, and incredibly the Royal Mail delivered approximately 750 million Christmas cards. On one amazing day on 15 December 2008, the Royal Mail delivered an incredible 123 million cards, so no wonder the Queen uses them.

The charity Mind ran an online poll that found half of all people felt they had spent more on Christmas than they could afford. Some 33 per cent would take six months to clear their credit cards and the accountants Deloittes found that the 2007 average family Christmas spend was £712. Even more worrying were the Children's Mutual Fund findings in December 2007 which found that the average child owns 1,720 toys during their childhood – why then, you wonder, do they need to be bought more? If you are worrying about all that space you might need, there is brighter news as 41 per cent of toys and presents given at Christmas are broken or lost by March.

Each year the Toy Retailers Association announces its 'Toy of the Year' and a review of the winners over the last 30 years highlights how society has changed. In the early 1980s the Rubik's Cube ruled and today you would buy these once-sought-after toys in pound shops or throw them into the Secret Santa at work. The 1980s also included the triumphant era of Transformers and Sylvania Families. The 1990s brought with it the new era of must-have expensive gadget toys such as the Nintendo Game Boy. However, one stalwart did triumph in 1996 when that old diva, Barbie, won Toy of the Year. Needless to say the new millennium saw more technology, higher costs and increasing waiting lists of must-have gifts: Xboxes, iPods, the Sony PlayStation Portable and Wii. Where will all this end? Possibly with the world's latest Sony Virtual Christmas PlayStation where you don't even need to have Christmas, just enjoy a virtual experience on your PlayStation. Oh dear, that will be virtually the end of Merry Christmas. When it comes to Christmas presents our meteoric progress to emotional enlightenment is exemplified by the most used phrase on Christmas Day: 'Do you have the receipt?'

We seem to have lost so many of our wonderful Christmas traditions and one of these was the rather fetching race to become the Christmas Number One. It's no longer a race but rather a wait to see who Simon Cowell chooses, or more accurately who wins the December final of *The X Factor*, although that was until the 2009 rebellion. Do you remember the great duels of the past such as Wizzard versus Slade (which, as we all know, Slade won) or more recently Darkness versus Gary Jules ('Mad World')? The list of former Christmas Number Ones is a wonderful litany of great songs and performers; 'Another Brick in the Wall' (Pink Floyd), 'Don't you Want Me' (Human League), 'Stay Another Day' (East 17), 'I Will Always Love You' (Witney Houston), 'Do They Know It's Christmas' (Band Aid 1984), 'Moon River' (Danny Williams), 'I Want to Hold Your Hand' (The Beatles) and of course 'Merry Xmas Everybody' (Slade).

Both The Beatles and Cliff Richard have had four Christmas Number Ones, although Cliff cleverly spread it around, two solos, one with The Shadows and one with Band Aid 20. The Spice Girls notched up three consecutive Number Ones and Queen managed it twice with 'Bohemian Rhapsody', in 1975 and 1991. It's a shame such a tradition is being lost, although before we get too melancholy it's worth remembering some experiences best left behind: 'Can We Fix It' (Bob the Builder), 'Two Little Boys' (Rolf Harris), 'Save Your Love' (Renée and Renato) and worst of all – 'Mr Blobby'.

Another dying tradition is the TV blockbuster on Christmas Day, although to be fair we will still have plenty of festive soap opera deaths to anticipate. Have you noticed how the soap opera producers tease everyone along in December leading up to the inevitable death, major violent or sexual assault in the Christmas Day episode – oh how that gives you a warm feeling inside!

Christmases past included the much anticipated specials that you just couldn't see any other time of the year. A look back in time reminds us of these huge events: 1977 *Morecombe and Wise Christmas Special* (30.1 million viewers), 1996 *Only Fools and Horses* (24.3 million) and of course in 1986 Den handing Ange her divorce papers, 'This, my sweet, is a letter from my solicitor telling you that your husband has filed for divorce – Happy Christmas, Ange.'

The 2008 Christmas top show was at least a return to family viewing with Wallace and Gromit (*A Matter of Loaf and Death*) but with an audience of only 14.3 million – how times have changed. With the age of Sky Plus, DVDs, iPods and the Internet you can watch what you want, when you want; progress – perhaps, just change – definitely.

A Christmas tradition that is also slowly withering away is the office Christmas party and for this we can thank those fun chums of the European Union and employment law. The Forum of Private Business said that warnings to employers were scaring them into cancelling office parties. The main problem is that the Christmas party is covered by the same laws as those in the workplace. You can no more kiss the boss, photocopy your rear end, pat Miss Jones's backside or put laxatives in the water cooler at the Christmas party, than you can on a normal day at work. Therefore, ACAS warns us that raffling a bottle of champagne could offend Muslim employees or modern music could upset older workers and, best of all, all decorations must undergo health-and-safety assessments. Unfortunately, all perspective is lost and we can't differentiate between a drunken boss putting his hand up a secretary's skirt (bad) and the credit control department dancing to 'YMCA' (fun)!

In December 2005 Canon, the digital imaging technology company, reported that their own independent national research had shown that 32 per cent of technicians called out at Christmas found broken glass from photocopiers being sat on or paper jams that revealed embarrassing images! According to Canon, amongst the more bizarre items found in a photocopier were a sleeping cat, a sausage roll, a condom, stockings, a vibrator, a cheque for £6,000 and a snake – in fact, all you need for a great party.

I believe Christmas works best when it is simple and traditional; spent with your close family in friendly, comfortable and familiar surroundings, enjoying the best food and wine you can afford, doing it the traditional way and doing the things you don't normally do during the rest of the year such as playing board games, wearing silly hats at dinner, listening to Slade, being nice to each other and eating dates. Incidentally, do you know of anyone who eats dates other than at Christmas?

One of those once-a-year extravagances is the indomitable Christmas cracker and the £25 million we spend each year on these anomalies and their stunning jokes: 'How can you get your name in lights the world over?' Answer – 'Change your name to Emergency Exit!' The jokes are very often less than perfectly PC but they still seem to survive, which brings us suitably to the next subject: political correctness.

7

I Shouldn't Have Said That

Christmas will soon be banned and replaced by the Festive Season; that is if the Political Correctness people get their way, though perhaps I shouldn't have said that in case I might possibly have offended someone!

Political correctness itself is in danger of becoming a clichéd term, although as far as many people are concerned, it's already crossed the boring threshold. Politically correct can be summarised to mean, 'The practice of using speech that conforms to liberal opinion by avoiding language which might cause offence to, or disadvantage social minorities.' The term is said to derive from the Marxist-Leninist vocabulary to describe the party line. For the bored majority it now means: 'The practice of completely losing any semblance of common sense or a mature perspective.'

The concept of political correctness (PC) evolved in the 1970s as part of the drive by US feminists to deal with discrimination against women. The feminists clearly achieved their objectives because today if I hear a dog described as 'man's best friend', I feel some guilt on behalf of our previous culture for its charming but antique prejudice. The phrase political correctness was coined by John Sullivan III in 1988, during an after-dinner speech, complaining about how Black Americans were being allowed to take the jobs traditionally reserved for the white majority. John Sullivan was allegedly a member of the Ku Klux Klan, so as far as I'm concerned, if *he* didn't like political correctness, then there must be something worthwhile in it.

When I was a young child I was given many words of wisdom from my parents, including, 'Sticks and stones may break your bones, but words will never harm you.' I heard what my parents said but all those years ago when I was being verbally bullied in the playground I have to admit that their fine advice didn't seem to help too much. However, as an adult I now see that if the deliverer intends offence, the tonality and framework of what they say will support their intention, and if they don't intend to upset the recipient, it generally won't; that was, until political correctness arrived on the scene.

A local authority gave some helpful politically correct guidelines to their staff when they suggested there was no such thing as failure, but rather 'deferred success', which I really like. You see, PC does make you feel better, as who wouldn't prefer a deferred success to a dismal catastrophic failure?

Who is it that actually decides what is correct? At the present moment the political left seem to be in ownership of this right to decide what is correct, with the media delighted also to play their part. However, the political right have also taken up the mantle and there is just as strong an ownership by them of the 'what is not correct about PC', as there is by the political left over, 'what is correct about political correctness'. Given that we now have a government with a right and a left, who knows what fun awaits us! The battle lines are drawn, emotions are running high and to hedge their bets the media supports both sides and all this over some words.

You can really have fun with this new correct way of talking and the following are some words with a reframed PC Cleansing Proposal, designed to avoid any chance at all of possibly causing offence to anyone, in any situation, or perhaps not: operation changed to 'direct health intervention' – just in case you are a pacifist; dishonest changed to 'ethically challenged' – just in case you are a liar; ignorant changed to 'factually unaware' – just in case you are dumb or rude; dead changed to 'life deficient' – just in case one word won't do. However, the very act of listing these suggestions may result in me achieving another deferred success, as I may have caused offence to the anti-political correctness people; in which case, I'm clearly not being politically correct. Phew, complicated, isn't it?

The book *Animal Farm* by George Orwell concludes with the pigs, who have taken over the farm from the humans, actually evolving into humans. The human resources (HR) industry has avidly taken up the cause of political correctness, I'm sure for no other reason than to avoid litigation against their masters. However, in HR terms the pigs are well on the way to becoming humans, which is evidenced by a staff member (sorry, team member) complaining about the term 'human resources' because 'they are not a resource, they are a person'. The underlying implication of the complainant is that HR people carefully nurture and develop their resources, treating them like a crop, ready to harvest at the appropriate time, suggesting a form of genetic engineering in the workplace. You can't please everyone and in any event what was wrong with 'Personnel'?

If one intends offence, one's actions are offensive, and if one does not intend offence, it is at worst ill-informed. The *Collins Essential English Dictionary* definition of giving offence is 'To cause to feel upset or angry'. If those primary school playground bullies came to me today and apologised and explained they didn't mean anything, I would feel much better and, if they didn't, I might give them what they deserve. Oh dear, another deferred success!

Because the world seems to have become hypersensitive, we appear to have a PC story in the media every week. Incidentally, I love the way the media play both sides. One week they are mocking the latest crazy PC decision made by some public body, such as a local school deciding to ban Nativity plays at Christmas in case it offends children of non-Christian religions and the next week they are castigating a Home Office minister for using the term 'nitty-gritty'. I would like to wager that you do not know why the phrase 'Nitty-gritty' could be considered offensive and yet John Denham, back then (in 2002) a Home Office minister, was castigated for his casual use of the term, although of course today politicians are much more careful than they were back in the early days of PC.

It has been loosely suggested that the term 'nitty-gritty' refers to the debris that was left in the bottom of slave ships at the end of a voyage. Dr Jonathan Lighter, then editor of the *Historical Dictionary of American Slang*, records the first example of its use as being in 1956 and therefore any offence is at the very best extremely tenuous and probably unfounded. How could Mr Denham possibly have intended offence when it is almost certain he didn't know of this very loose and unproven connection with an historical event? It has also been suggested that the word 'picnic' derives from a slave-lynching party. If we carry on like this everyone will be speaking in sentences of fewer than five words, followed of course by a disclaimer and conversation will then definitely not be a picnic!

One of my favourite pieces of enlightened HR politically correct advice is to 'steer clear of birthday cards in the workplace that make fun of people's ages in case they get upset'. Presumably the birthday boy or girl does actually know their own age and has at least retained some sense of humour. The very worst result would be that they don't find the card funny and then who would look a fool for their insensitivity? Without doubt it is the giver for not knowing the recipient well enough. It's just plain common sense and insensitive people have always been boorish and they always will be. Surely, mature people don't need protecting from everyday life?

This political correctness will mean we get more occurrences such as the example of rewriting Shakespeare in the form of *Romeo and Julian*, an alternative gay version of *Romeo and Juliet*; advice by a local council not to use the words 'policeman', 'fireman' or 'chairman' because they are classic examples of exclusionary language; rewrites of the words of the 'Drunken Sailors' sea shanty; rejection by a government agency of the admittedly violent 'Three Little Pigs' fairy tale because it raises cultural issues; and, best of all, banning the book *Animal Farm* because it might offend some minorities as it includes pigs. Have any of the PC people actually read this book: it's a farm, which includes various animals, including pigs, as pigs are often on farms, and its powerful message is well worth reading, especially for politically correct people. It's for this reason that the book has been on the syllabus of school exam boards for over 40 years and will undoubtedly continue to outlast this PC craze.

Political correctness is becoming dangerous because its broad banner stifles any meaningful debate on some very important social issues. In this country we need to have an open debate regarding racial, sexual, ageist and religious prejudice and political correctness stops this. We are in danger of a black-and-white scenario where one is seen as either on the one hand as liberal, bureaucratically politically correct and unrealistic, or on the other hand as reactionary, politically incorrect and full of common sense. This lazy thinking could easily get in the way of a meaningful debate about important social issues such as female genital mutilation, homophobia, the value of Christmas as a British cultural event not just a religious celebration for Christians, freedom of speech and many more vital matters for society to face up to and deal with.

Judging people by the colour of their skin, their age, their religion, their sexual inclination, how they look or their gender is clearly prejudicial – surely the world would be a better place if we all judged each other simply by our actions and behaviours? If we treat each other like adults, you never know we might regain our sense of humour. 'Praise be' to whatever you believe in.

On the bright side, although PC does somewhat extend sentences, it can provide some real benefits, as there is great appeal in my beer gut becoming my 'hop storage facility', moaning becoming 'repetitive vocal under-appreciation' and nagging becoming 'orally consistent constructive criticism'. This offers endless possibilities for bad behaviour to become more acceptable: a miser becomes a 'person of cautiously negative generosity'; laziness becomes 'motivational active deficiency'; BO becomes 'non-hygienic environmental disorder'; being boring becomes 'inactive non-engagement behaviour'; ogling becomes 'compulsive intrusive sensual focus' and, best of all in our modern often mildly obese lives, overeating becomes 'reverse bulimia'!

One area of contemporary life where a particular type of behaviour and speech hasn't yet come under the PC spotlight is swearing. Everywhere you go today swearing is on the increase in places where it was previously unheard of: in movies as a standard protocol, in books and, of course, on TV. We have reached the situation where it's notable if a comedian *doesn't* swear. People of my generation will describe the quality of a comedian using, as one of their main criteria, the fact that they 'didn't swear'. The argument goes that there is an array of alternative adjectives available to gain the required impact without swearing.

When you consider this, there are very few swear words: we have the nasty f word, the horrendous c word, one s word and two b words and beyond this you are into the weird and obscure world of swearing, where only aficionados go. Thus there are only five real swear words, which isn't bleeping many. Admittedly, a swear word is just a collection of bleeping letters which for some bleeping historical cultural reason is considered to be bleeping indiscreet or uncouth.

One swear word that's found itself out on the edge of acceptable is 'bloody' and so much so that I can feel comfortable about actually spelling it out in full. Bloody has done pretty well for itself, running a successful and independent acceptability spin campaign, and certainly other swear words like the f word would do well to follow it, but I hope not.

As we know, political correctness creates all manner of controversy and much heated debate. Of course we need to be sensitive to others' needs, especially minority groups who don't have the necessary muscle to defend themselves, and in my opinion that's one of the key attributes of a civilised society. However, it's also particularly unhealthy to get so earnest about such things that we lose our ability to laugh at ourselves and therefore don't regularly question our values. Surely it must be politically correct to poke fun at political correctness and celebrate the fact that we are free to do so?

Our press have an important part to play in the protection of freedom, although at the moment they are having far too much fun playing both sides against each other in the PC debate, which brings us suitably to the next subject: the media.

8

It Has Been Reported

I have a suspicion that political correctness was a media invention and, if not, then at the very least the media has avidly embraced the concept because political correctness alone regularly fills large amounts of column space in newspapers and on news websites.

The media plays an important role in a free society, although this does have some disadvantages: we can't have freedom of speech without a few less than savoury matters being uncovered; we can't have instant access to the Internet without easy access to some vile pornography; we can't have wall-to-wall choice of TV channels without inevitably a significant dose of dross as well; we can't be fascinated by the rich and famous without being fed a diet of celebrity nonsense; we can't have instant communication without instant access and no censorship; we can't be rubberneckers of trauma without being fed negativity here, there and everywhere; and of course famous sportsmen can't use the media to build their fame and fortune and then complain when the media turns against them when they sleep with a prostitute who is a grandmother. This seems remarkably unfair because of the obvious fact that topping up another citizen's pension must be a socially aware activity.

In a free country that embraces freedom of speech and doesn't just pay it lip service, the media will always be a source of great power and we probably get the media that we as a society deserve. This media influence was never clearer than when the then most powerful man in the world was brought down by two journalists in Washington and his name, of course was Richard Nixon, and the scandal Watergate. With great power comes great responsibility and this is where we might suggest that the media perhaps doesn't always deliver.

In World War II the British media were very responsible and generally gave out careful versions of events that were just about truthful but always veering on the side of a positive spin to quite properly help the British cause, although one could argue they had little choice, as the government were effectively controlling all important output. Imagine the headlines and the deadly effect upon public morale if today's media was let loose unfettered on those World War II stories: 'Disaster at Dunkirk – the Bosch smash us into the sea'; 'We can't take any more – London's Blitz takes us to the limit of endurance'; or 'We're doomed – every Spitfire in the air'. Thank goodness no one published these headlines, as I have a strong feeling that, if they did, we probably wouldn't be here now to reflect upon this freely.

The media is thought to have started with the Chinese Tang Dynasty where news was handwritten on silk. In Beijing as far back as 1582 there is the first reference to privately published news leaflets and it's both fascinating and ironic that the freedom of the press started its embryonic journey in the very place that today is attacked by the Western press for its lack of free speech.

In 1609 the first daily paper, *A-visa*, was published in Augsburg, Germany, and you could say this was a passport to today's mayhem! John Milton's pamphlet 'Areopagitica, a Speech for Liberty of Unlicensed Printing', which was published in 1644, was one of the first pieces of media putting the case for freedom of the press. Following the invention of the printing press, the early use of printing equipment was restricted to a small group, which isn't very different from today where a small number of newspaper publishers reign supreme. In 1814 *The Times* of London acquired a printing press capable of making 1,100 impressions a minute and thus the madness started.

The *Guinness Book of Records* states that the Soviet newspaper *Trud* had a circulation of 21.5 million, which is an awful lot of newspapers to sell in one day. The UK's top seller is the *Sun* at 3.1 million (2008) while the niche *Financial Times* sells approximately 417,000, although I'm pretty sure 400,000 of these are left on commuter trains! Amazingly the English-language newspaper the *Times of India* outsells *The Times* in the UK threefold.

At the time of writing, *The Sun* newspaper is supreme with the highest circulation numbers. It was first published in 1964, surprisingly enough originally as a broadsheet. However, in 1969 Rupert

Murdoch took over the newspaper and converted *The Sun* into a tabloid. The first model to show her breasts on 'page three' was in 1970 and the newspaper's progress (not without a few boobs along the way) has continued until today. *The Sun* is famous for its often outrageous punning headlines, especially during the Falklands War; 'Gotcha!' regarding the sinking of the *Belgrano* and 'Stick it up your Junta!'

In May 2009 the newspaper received official praise when the Poet Laureate, Carol Ann Duffy, aged 53, lesbian mother of one (as reported in *The Sun* of course), had some very positive words to say about *The Sun*. She said, '*The Sun*'s headlines are an example of how poetry can be accessible to everyone'; Sir John Betjeman – gotcha!

The newspaper has previously had an enormous effect upon political trends, famously supporting Margaret Thatcher to help win the 1979 general election. The late Sir Larry Lamb, the *Sun*'s first editor used the phrase 'Winter of Discontent', which so heavily influenced political thinking during that time. Other tabloids followed and notably during the George Michael arrest in the USA for lewd behaviour in a public toilet, they all had great schoolboy giggly fun with: 'Zip Me Up before You Go-Go' by *The Sun* and 'Wham Bam Flash in the Pan', the *Daily Star*. George, although still in the news for the wrong reasons, may have the last laugh, though, because he is still doing world tours to ever-increasing audiences while newspaper circulation numbers continue to fall.

It is a fact that newspaper circulation is going down and 'it has been reported' that this is because of the Internet and freely available online news. Despite this you have to admit newspapers have so much to offer us and we mustn't let the Internet win this particular battle. For instance, you can't make a paper plane out of a Dell. Without a newspaper you can't easily start a cosy log fire in a country pub; *Blue Peter* would not have existed without newsprint as a key ingredient of paper-mâché, plus, of course, as all Valerie Singleton fans know, flour and water; no kidnapper worth their salt could send terrifying messages to the victim's family without something from which to cut those little letters and, lest we forget, when the Andrex runs out, what else can do the trick to deal with your big job.

If you are not a great newspaper reader, a piece of news will always eventually find you, via the Internet, through headlines blasted out at you from railway station plasmas, rolling news headlines or by a family member saying to you, 'Have you heard about …?'

Whether you like newspapers or not, have you noticed that you have a form of compulsion to pick up a newspaper when you see one lying around? You can't stop yourself and when you see a newspaper you just have to read it, don't you? If I find a discarded *Financial Times* lying on the seat next to me on a train, all screwed up, used and dumped by its previous owner, all forlorn, abused and abandoned, just crying out for attention – I pick it up! Despite the thoughts in my mind of the germs left on the newsprint by its previous unknown owner, I just have to pick it up and partake of 'mucky seconds'. I can't seem to control this compulsion. It is possible that, if the government banned secondary use of news-papers, it would completely eradicate the common cold from our country.

One of the many great British traditions that is in sad decline is that of the paperboy or papergirl. A Halifax survey of children's finances found that in 2004 one-third of 7 to 16-year-olds who worked did so with a paper round. In 2007 this figure was down by approximately a half and one of the main reasons may well be that children today receive too much pocket money. Who would want to get up at 5.30 a.m. and trudge around the dark cold streets with a heavy weight on your shoulders, when you could sit on your back-side watching a *Big Brother* rerun and be paid by your parents to do this?

During the height of the credit crunch furore I flew back across the Atlantic and on entering the plane was offered a newspaper. I hesitated but then gave in, having been abroad for a week and as a result was feeling somewhat sentimental about the Old Country. The newspaper was full of dire warnings about the finances of the country and the forthcoming budget. I soaked up the range of 'worst in 60 years' statements and felt decidedly depressed and my whole mood became downbeat. I decided there and then that reading newspapers was bad for my emotional well-being; that is, of course, until I next found a discarded *Financial Times* on the train.

Newspapers can err towards the negative and I suggest you might test this out yourself. Buy a popular tabloid and then with a pen in your hand mark up the articles and news stories which you consider offer a negative slant. Compare this to those stories with a positive slant. I guarantee that the ratio of negatives to positives is over five to one. In fact, it is likely you will have to reach at least page six before you get a positive story at all. In life this just isn't representative of how it is, where things are pretty much 50:50 and most people are generally honest and decent; in essence, as we know, in life you get the rough and you get the smooth.

This is the problem with newspapers, in that they pander to our fears, and really we all need to be encouraged, not discouraged. I remember hearing the news some years ago on the radio as I drove from my largest personal investment, my house: 'House prices have crashed again last month.' When I listened to the substance of the report it said that the rate of increase had dropped substantially from the previous month's rate of increase. By any definition, a drop in the rate of increase is not a crash. I know a few years later we subsequently entered a unique period of house price reductions, but the point is that at the time house prices were rising, but the presentation by the news headline was that there was a fall, in fact a crash. Facts can always be presented and framed in such a way as to mean something else and newspapers do this all the time, presenting opinion as fact.

Can you imagine a few of the best moments in life and then think of how a sharp editor could reframe these for the news: 'Not many good nights' sleep for a while' – the birth of your children; 'Enjoy it while you can' – your football team winning the FA Cup for the one and only time; 'This could go badly wrong'– when you set up your first business; 'Divorces cost a fortune' – on the eve of your marriage; 'Now do you feel old?' – the birth of your first grandchild. These headlines would not add anything to the enjoyment of your life and in fact would be an affront to these wonderful experiences, and that's why I avoid newspapers, unless of course they are discarded by someone else.

Libel is a major issue for publishers and from 2006 to 2008 the number of cases settled out of court doubled. Interestingly, the number of libel cases featuring celebrities has doubled to 32 per cent of all such claims. The *News of the World* fell foul of such a claim when Justin Timberlake won his case on 24 August 2005, disputing that he had cheated on his then girlfriend, Cameron Diaz. At face value it all sounds somewhat trivial. However, imagine your own situation if it was reported in a national newspaper that you had cheated on your spouse and you knew you hadn't. You would be very unhappy; although I'm not sure I would give my substantial damages to charity as Mr Timberlake did. Be honest, would you?

Article 10 of the European Convention on Human Rights permits restrictions on freedom of speech which are necessary for the protection of the reputation or the rights of others, and long may this continue. There is one exception, though, and that is parliamentary privilege, which I assume means Gordon Brown can say what he wants about you, but you can't say anything about him. Just ask Jeremy Clarkson!

The Romans had laws against defamation and their *convicium contra bonos mores* law is strangely paralleled by U2's action against a former stylist who was found by the Irish courts to have taken lead singer Bono's cowboy hat and, although according to U2's spokesperson proceedings were taken as a last resort, they do bring back those ancient *contra bonos mores* laws.

Aren't magazines an interesting concept and they certainly last a lot longer than newspapers? I find it a quaint experience reading about 'Hampshire's Best Christmas Recipes' on a sizzling-hot June afternoon while I wait for my six-monthly dental check-up. I would like to know how the magazines actually get into the surgery. Is the key requirement to work at a dentist's practice to have an interest in photography, as how else could you explain the preponderance of *Photography Today*s in every waiting room? Is there a place where you can lodge unwanted magazines and then practice administrators wander around these establishments carefully selecting ancient back copies of magazines to take back to the surgery waiting room? I would be very attracted to a surgery where the magazines were relevant, up-to-date and extensive. The time waiting for your personal dental torture would pass much more quickly. Surely any practice could stretch to the £30 a month in subscriptions needed to have a relevant and up-to-date magazine portfolio?

Alternatively, how about a new doctors' surgery magazine called *The Waiting Room*, designed for one purpose, and one purpose only, and that is to entertain patients while they wait to be seen? It could include advertisements about relevant products such as pile creams, sleeping potions, walking sticks, assorted ointments, creams and sprays, antacids, anti-allergy tablets and, how could we miss it out, Viagra? There could be useful articles on 'How to tell your doctor you have a problem getting aroused', 'What to do when you find yourself sat next to someone in the waiting room with bad BO' or 'How to deal with a dragon-lady practice receptionist'. The crossword could include only health issues, the horoscope could predict your next ache or pain, you could read about 'Ten simple tips on how to get the best deals on prescriptions' and the recipes would only include healthy salads. It certainly sounds like a magical mixture to me.

Of the top 50 magazine titles in the UK, three-quarters are published by just six publishers. When researching magazine circulation numbers, one thing is clear — women read more magazines than children or men. The figures for the six months to December 2008 showed the well-known women's magazines of *Cosmopolitan* at 450,836, *Woman and Home* at 353,160 and *Marie Claire* at 314,259, whereas the high-flying *FHM* for men comes in only at 272,545 and stands alone as a men's magazine with such high ratings. Speciality magazines like *Homes and Gardens* have circulation figures of 140,264 and one old favourite, *NME*, is at 48,459. However, the TV listing magazines of *TV Choice* at 1,369,088 and *Radio Times* at 1,023,255 shows that, as usual, TV rules.

Not one of these best-selling magazines, but I'm sure a high-quality read, is *The Marquetarian*, first produced in 1952 and the veritable mainstay of the Marquetry Society. According to their website, 99 per cent of the magazines are never thrown away, which would explain why you never see a copy in a doctor's waiting room.

There are magazines published that cover subjects that are varied, specialist and sometimes off-the-wall. One magazine that particularly catches the eye is a title dedicated to conspiracy theories or, more specifically, to the investigation of, in its own words, 'state espionage, government conspiracies, the abuse of government power and the influence of the intelligence and security agencies on contemporary history and politics' – wow! This magazine is called *Lobster, the Journal of Para-Politics*, which proudly boasted on its website, 'As denounced in the House of Commons'. Surely, above all else, this proves we do live in a free country as there are places in the world where this would not be allowed without a chilling midnight visit from the authorities? Rule Britannia!

If you're in the media you need to catch people's attention and the best way to achieve this is through a great headline. Unfortunately, sometimes journalists just try too hard and the following are actual newspaper headlines from around the world. 'Something Went Wrong in Jet Crash, Expert Says' – that's what I call an expert! 'British Union Finds Dwarfs in Short Supply' – that's definitely not PC. 'Iraqi Head Seeks Arms' – soon he will have the complete package. 'Plane Too Close to Ground, Crash Probe Told' – how much did this investigation cost? 'Prostitutes Appeal to Pope' – now that's a surprise. 'Red Tape Holds up Bridge' – that duct tape is wonderful. 'War Dims Hope of Peace' – shame. 'Stolen Painting Found by Tree' – I hope its reward was a good pruning.

The days of the great newspaper headlines are soon to be over due to the growing use by newspapers of Internet sites. It isn't enough to have a catchy and clever attention-grabbing headline as you now need a headline that works in Search Engine Optimisation (SEO). As a result we may return to the style before the 1960s of simple factual headlines. These are examples of some historic and yet simple headlines from the twentieth century: 'Greatest Crash in Wall Street's History' – *Daily Mail*, 25 October 1929; 'Hitler Dead' – *News Chronicle*, 2 May 1945; 'The Space Dog Lives' – *Daily Mail*, 4 November 1957, about Curly, the Soviet Union's first space dog.

When surfing news sites on the Web, my own favourite is the BBC's. It seems 'tradition and brand' do still count for something. The BBC News Website itself has contained some memorable headlines: 'Mince Pie Danger to be Assessed' – an article about a village Christmas party needing a council risk assessment which memorably includes the quotation, 'I also understand Santa may need a criminal records bureau check' – brilliant. Another gem is 'Turkish Airline Gets the Hump' – an article that covers Turkish Airlines staff going too far when they sacrificed a camel in celebration at Istanbul International Airport and apparently 700 kilograms of camel meat was distributed to workers. That's the last meat sandwich I buy at an airport.

My favourite headline is 'Drunk Darth Vader Spared Jail', which appeared in May 2008 and, without disrespecting the obvious discomfort to the victim of this attack, we must rejoice in the statement from Judge Shaw: 'There had been an element of premeditation in the assaults, because he had been wearing the black bin bag.' What a give-away, Luke!

So much of our media is now full of the rich and famous and in today's modern world it is virtually impossible to achieve fame and fortune without the media on your side, which brings us suitably to the next subject: celebrities.

9

I Want to Be Famous

The media often makes or breaks people and TV, closely followed by the press, has the power to make someone famous overnight or destroy them. Unfortunately, society seems plagued by evil people who will do anything to become notorious and it is true, but obscene, that one simple but terrifying way to achieve this notoriety is to become a serial killer.

It's drastic, vile and immoral but it will almost certainly make you instantly famous, so thank goodness you also need to be insane. Noel Gallagher of Oasis said, '*X Factor* causes winners instant mental illness.' Perhaps this time he has a point, and there is some comfort in knowing that *The X Factor* might save many innocent people who would otherwise be victims of fame-seeking serial killers.

It's easy to be famous but surely a sane individual isn't prepared to give so much away to gain notoriety? Thank goodness for society the answer is 'No', although there is a worrying trend building where people will perform increasingly bizarre activities just to become famous, especially on YouTube. Presumably this is the reason why streakers run naked on to rugby or cricket pitches to have just five minutes of fame, at whatever cost and however unimpressive their display!

Celebrities influence our lives and reflect and define our culture, and therefore by definition celebrities need to be famous. However, is being a celebrity just about fame or does it require great wealth, success and huge talent? It seems that the answer is any one or all of these. 'Celebrity' seems to be a creation of the media and it is because we live in a world of instant communication that the public cannot get enough of celebrities' lives. Believe it or not, we once had things called newspapers that included news of ordinary people and boring old world events.

Nowadays it's an easy fill-in of space for a magazine or newspaper to purchase a celebrity's wedding photograph or buy an article from a PR agent. We live in a media world where a picture of Davina McCall pregnant was reportedly sold for £7,500! I am the first to agree that pregnant women look rather fetching and natural, and of course Davina is a particularly attractive woman. However, to pay 38 per cent of the annual average net wage of ordinary people in this country for a picture of one of the 568,500 women who were pregnant in the country at that time is extraordinary and possibly a distorted perspective of what really matters in life.

It has been reported that the parents of the Brangelina Twins, Vivienne Marcheline and Knox Leon, sold their first pictures of the twins for $14 million. In case you didn't know, these babies' parents are William Bradley Pitt and Angelina Jolie. Brad and Angelina then reportedly donated all this money to charity, which is a very generous gesture, because however wealthy they both are, it's still a significant sum of money to give to a good cause. The surprising thing is that the pictures were seen as being worth $14 million, but quite clearly there was a demand and this was the market price. To put this into perspective, for $14 million you could probably buy Lewis Hamilton's Monaco apartment, David Beckham, Costa Coffee's chief coffee taster's tongue (actually the insurance value of it), or Botticelli's 1470 masterpiece *St Francis and the Angels*. Which would you use your $14 million to buy? I'm guessing not the baby pictures.

Jennifer Lopez (Cleopatra?) and husband, Marc Anthony, were reportedly suing the British pram company Silver Cross for a staggering £3.5 million for allegedly using a picture of their daughter in one of their prams to promote the pram. I believe it would be very prudent to make no further comments on this as we wouldn't relish a lawsuit from the parents! However, Silver Cross made their name when the Queen purchased a pram for Prince Charles to sleep in, and I am assuming our monarch didn't receive any money for this and certainly didn't sue anyone. I should just make it clear (for no other reason than to avoid legal action) that this was 60 years ago, as Prince Charles has long since grown out of it.

Jennifer Aniston was reported as having once said, 'I want to be happy and loved, and not settling for something I think is second best and less than I deserve.' These are admirable words, although they do sound somewhat like the self-motivational words anyone of my daughters' friends might say to themselves after a 'messy' relationship break-up. This probably proves that celebrities are not immune from the same old day-to-day challenges we all face.

There is, of course, the latest form of instant celebrity contact which is called Twittering. It is an extension of chatroom-style networking forums like MySpace whereby people post short messages of under 140 characters on to a micro-blogging site. Needless to say in today's world, mobile phones are the most used medium. Twittering is attractive because of its intimacy and ease of use. Many celebrities now post on Twitters and for ordinary people it must be great to feel like John Cleese is personally contacting you on New Year's Eve to say, 'Happy New Year everyone, and may your New Year's flatulence be tuneful and fragrantly inoffensive.' I wouldn't hold your breath for a reply though! In January 2009 the most powerful man in the world (not Bill Gates but President Barack Obama) became the then most popular person on Twitter with 144,000 followers. Is there a connection?

Most celebrities now have blogs and this title was derived from the coinage 'Web-log'. Have you noticed how today we seem to love acronyms or, as I like to call them, FLAWs (meaning Four Letter Acronym Words)? Virtually every celebrity has a site and Laurence Llewelyn-Bowen is no exception and it's well worth a visit. Try visiting it while he is away, colour it purple and see how he likes it.

Just a click away there is a whole world of enlightening information ready for us all and within seconds you could be on your favourite celebrity's blog receiving his or her insights into the meaning of life. Through this medium you are now able to connect with every one of your much loved celebrities and catch up with their latest thoughts on virtually anything. Without these blogs you would miss entries like Paris Hilton's blog entry of 16 March 2009: 'It's so amazing here (her hotel), there's even a bowling alley in my room.' This is all very exciting, but tragically there was no sign of there being a dominoes set.

Our whole world is now so full of celebrity information that *Celebrity* has become an industry in itself. When researching the array of celebrity websites I was astonished by the extraordinary sites with very specific areas of interest. The following caught my eye and I'm sure are well worth a visit: 'Most Expensive Celebrity Divorces' – when will they learn; 'All Things Diva' – unfortunately the *i* in 'Things' isn't a typographical error as of course I had to check; Celebrity Car Parade – lots of blacked-out windows; 'Celebrity Toys' – the mind boggles (sponsored by Ann Summers?); 'Celebs on Crack' – plenty of material there; 'Whatever Happened To' – inevitably, because fame doesn't always last; and, amazingly, 'Celebs Missing Fingers' – honestly, hands up, there *is* such a site.

Disability doesn't seem to be a real barrier to fame and success; there are many notable people who have had to overcome physical challenges included in history's Hall of Fame: Stephen Hawking (of course), Lord Nelson, John Milton (he was blind when he wrote *Paradise Lost*), Beethoven (incredibly he suffered from deafness) and Albert Einstein, who had a learning disability, did not speak until aged three and had difficulty at school with maths.

I am an admirer of Kate Winslet for a number of reasons, primarily because she is a fine actress, but also because she has strong objections to what could be referred to as the bulimic style of fashion, plus she seems to be what can best be described as grounded. Needless to say, I don't know her and have never actually met her one-to-one and like most people I just engage with her onscreen persona. When I put in a search on Google for Kate Winslet, 14,606,000 sites were found, so I'm clearly not on my own! I had remembered reading in the news of a small difficulty Kate had with someone who wandered on to her property and therefore entered a search for 'Kate Winslet Angry' and was still offered 379,000 sites. The mind boggles at how this search could develop. The Internet really is a crazy thing.

Unlike Kate not all celebrities use their own birth name and it would make life much more straightforward if parents gave their newborns a name that could be used just in case they became famous, although Gordon Sumner's parents would have done well to come up with Sting.

I wonder whether Sting of Police fame looks in the mirror to buck himself up and says something like, 'Sting, now on Monday we will get down to cleaning up the garage.' Or does he think to himself, 'Gordon, on Monday I will get down to cleaning up the garage'? Sting's real name is Gordon Matthew Thomas Sumner and at what time in his life did Sting take over from Gordon, as this would explain a lot about what it means to be a celebrity?

When we are travelling together my wife often buys celebrity magazines such as *Heat*, *OK* and *Hello!*, because she says they are an easy read (although I would say 'easy view' is a better description) and help to pass the time on long journeys. We have a game we play called 'Know the Celeb' which involves her taking me through a magazine, page by page, to check my awareness of, first, the celebrity's name and, second, what they do, or have appeared in. If I know it I get one point, and if I don't and she does then my wife gains a point. I confess to being a very poor performer at this game, although I have noticed that practice does help. Recently, in one magazine we found a page whereby pictures of celebrities were marked with orange circles, as if a strident schoolmaster had got their hands on a giant orange marker pen and joyously ran riot, highlighting all the celebrities' physical imperfections.

I understand that such pages are common practice in many magazines. If by some strange quirk of fate you should become famous, aren't you frightened to imagine the type of orange saturated page you would get? It's best to look on the bright side (heavily orange in my case) and consider how helpful it would be to have every physical blemish and imperfection so carefully highlighted and then, thanks to the magazine, you could focus your attention on a particularly meaningful airbrush and plastic surgery campaign!

Being a celebrity must have very significant disadvantages, starting, of course, with the orange marker pen. Reporters now have all
the modern instant communication paraphernalia and a picture of a
celebrity drunk and being sick in the street taken on a mobile phone
by a passer-by can be on the Web within an hour. Now that *is*
progress.

The world we live in today is celebrity-mad and we can't seem to
get enough of the rich and famous. Everyone seems to be desperate for fame and fortune, but is it as obviously a beneficial ambition
as it first appears? Consider some of these downsides from being
wealthy and famous. Lack of privacy – you can't even be sick in the
street. You lose all engagement with real life and you can't even call
a national florist to buy a bouquet for your loved one and enjoy the
delights of going through all those levels of their automated telephone ordering system, as someone else does this for you. You
can't get that rush of excitement when your pay cheque arrives each
month because you don't get to worry about money at all. You can't
get that Monday-morning blues feeling, or Tuesday, or Wednesday,
or Thursday. You never know who your real friends are, especially
new acquaintances; do they love you or do they love your money
and fame? Still, it beats being poor!

Let's undertake a private experiment to explore this further.
All you have to do is use your memory and imagination. Please
remember a small number of events that have occurred during your
life, particularly those involving your more extreme behaviours,
difficulties and generally interesting interactions with others. Just
pause to collect these thoughts. Then imagine that any one of these
events is the subject of any or all of the following: a tell-all article in
a newspaper told by your ex-wife or ex-husband, ex-boyfriend or
girlfriend, ex-business partner or colleague, and written by a skilled,
tenacious and ruthless journalist; a magazine photograph of you
taken by the paparazzi from a distance and without your knowledge
or approval while in the process of an *interesting* event; something
you said in private (probably when slightly inebriated) being taken

out of context and quoted in the media as your beliefs; or worst of all a picture of you relaxed, away from it all, frolicking in the sea with your loved ones and letting it all hang out! How did you do with the experiment? Still want to be famous?

Some celebrities take many, many years to achieve their success. Sting is now a mature world-renowned musician with a long career of musical success covering a range of different styles of music. Do you remember his wilder younger days, on the edge of Punk, the days of Roxanne and the first successful albums? In actual fact, Sting's major breakthrough success came when he was 27 years old, after he had previously qualified and worked as a schoolteacher.

Mr William Bradley Pitt is fondly remembered by women the world over for his screen breakthrough in the movie *Thelma and Louise* playing a young toy boy scallywag who, amongst other things, enjoys urgently making love to and stealing money from Geena Davies; and of course Brad being a true gentleman does it in that order. This fresh-faced young star was actually 28 years old at the time, so clearly success really can take surprisingly long to achieve, even if you were born very pretty.

As part of the 2009 Red Nose Day we were able to enjoy a programme watching nine celebrities trek to the top of Mount Kilimanjaro. At the time of writing they were well on track to generating the highest-ever amount for a charity expedition, approaching £3.5 million, which is a magnificent effort. A former business partner of mine also climbed to the top of Kilimanjaro's 5,895 metres and he was very frank in saying that it was the hardest thing he had every done in his life and wouldn't be going back. However, the nine celebrities, of Fearne Cotton, Denise van Outen, Alesha Dixon, Cheryl Cole, Kimberley Walsh, Chris Moyles, Ronan Keating, Ben Shepherd and Gary Barlow, weren't on their own. The celebrity team were part of a group of 43 people and 500 kilograms of equipment. It seems there are some advantages in being a celebrity.

Despite my wife's celebrity knowledge and her desire to meet some famous people, it's me who occasionally inadvertently crosses paths with celebrities, and unfortunately never her. It's a strange thing in life that, when you don't try too hard, things just seem to happen. When you spend any time with famous people, complete strangers drop all decorum and approach you very directly and say things like 'Was that Dennis Waterman you were with?'

But beware, because there are dangers in being celebrity-blind. Once on a charity golf day I was sat at the dinner table after playing a round of golf and was having an enjoyable conversation with a charming man sitting next to me. I had one of those rare good days and was generous enough to offer my dinner guest an array of golfing tips, which he very politely accepted. When the prize-giving took place the compère said, 'We are very pleased to have with us today to give away the prizes, twice winner this year on the European Tour, Mr X.' You will not be surprised to learn that it was my co-dinner guest who rose to give the prizes. As he returned to the table having given away the prizes and delivered a very humorous speech, he gave me a friendly but knowing smile and I may have blushed.

However, this celebrity blindness can open the door to enjoyable exchanges that probably wouldn't be possible if one was blinded in the celeb headlights. When staying at the Waldorf Astoria in New York with my wife and two daughters, I found on checking in that the hotel had overbooked our rooms. As a result they kindly upgraded us to the only available room which was on the luxury floor. Unfortunately, I suffer from vertigo and the floor-to-ceiling window in the luxurious bathroom was too much for me. As I visited the toilet in the night with my back pressed against the wall to avoid the view of the 39-floor drop, I knew we had to move rooms and down. Needless to say, my family was not impressed when I moved us to a sixth-floor standard room for the rest of our stay. We moved all our belongings down the 33 floors only to find that my youngest daughter had left her bra and knickers in the luxury suite. Because they were still annoyed with me, my wife sent me up to the 39th floor as penance, to collect the underwear and then to visit reception on the ground floor and run another chore for her, a suitable punishment or so she thought.

I duly took this on the chin and entered the lift on the 39th floor with a fellow hotel guest and a lift attendant in residence. The lift was delayed and therefore I had a few minutes with my charming fellow guest. He was going to a charity event that evening and was dressed in black tie and tuxedo and, needless to say, I had to explain why I had a bra and panties in my hand. It was all very jolly and when my fellow guest left the lift for the limo area we bade each other a fond farewell. The lift attendant then very excitedly said to me, 'Do you know who that was? I said, 'No, sorry,' and he said, 'That was Tom Selleck.'

I have seen *Three Men and a Baby*, although I must admit I wasn't a *Magnum PI* fan. On that night, Tom (well, we're mates now) didn't have his trademark moustache, so I hope I am forgiven for not recognising him. My family were green with envy and my daughter now boasts that Monica's boyfriend, the dentist (*Friends*), has seen her underwear! If by any chance Tom Selleck gets to read this book, that unfazed and apparently overconfident man you met in the lift at the Waldorf Astoria, pretending not to be a cross-dresser, was me.

There is not necessarily a connection between wealth and fame but there is one between fame and wealth. In our media-driven world it would seem negligent to be famous and not to use this fame to gain great wealth. The UK's Rich List is compiled by the *Sunday Times* and every year gains considerable attention when it is released. The UK's 10 richest people in 2008 were all business magnates and I would suggest not many are household names: Lakshmi Mittal and family, Roman Abramovic, the Duke of Westminster, Sri and Gopi Hinuja, Alisher Usmanov, Ernesto and Kirsty Bertaelli, Hans Rausing and family, John Frederiksen, Sir Phillip and Lady Green, and David and Simon Reuben. Interestingly, the best known is probably Roman Abramovic, not famous for his wealth creation but famous for owning Chelsea Football Club.

However, in the Young People's Rich List there were quite a few well-known celebrities: Katie Price (£30 million), Jenson Button (£35 million), Michael Owen (£41 million), Wayne and Coleen Rooney (£35 million). No doubt because of their huge celebrity money-making status these figures are already well out of date. Coleen is a great example of wealth being used to create fame by systematically building up a brand, and good luck to her!

Calculating the richest people of all time by comparing their greatest personal wealth against the Gross Domestic Product (GDP) of their country of residence and roughly recalculating this wealth to reflect today's values surprisingly puts Bill Gates' wealth completely in the shade. The top two wealthiest people of all time, in terms of today's values, are considered to be John D. Rockefeller (approximately $330 billion) and Andrew Carnegie (approximately $300 billion). Both were men, which is hardly surprising given that their wealth was made in the nineteenth and early twentieth centuries. Both were from strict religious backgrounds, both had facial hair (moustache and beard) and both lived long lives (97 and 83) and so sadly it seems my best hope for great wealth and longevity rests with my beard. Not much of a plan really.

One other common trait was their philanthropy. John D. Rockefeller apparently gave away 10 per cent of his income every year and when he died in 1937 he had given away approximately 50 per cent of his wealth. Andrew Carnegie was an even more generous philanthropist, giving away the majority of his wealth. His family remain famous as a result of Carnegie Hall, the Carnegie Institute and a host of other long-standing legacies. This philanthropy would explain why the richest families at the turn of each century never appear again in the list at the turn of the next century. It seems extreme wealth is difficult to maintain across more than a couple of generations.

In fact, the examples of the Kilimanjaro climb and the lifetime gifts of the Carnegie family highlight how celebrities can use their fame to do good. Through my professional career I have known

Alan Titchmarsh for a number of years. A few years ago BBC's *Gardeners World* was being filmed at Alan's house in a garden at the top of his property. Both my parents were retired, keen gardeners and avid fans of Alan. My mum and dad have the same birthday and as a very special treat one year I asked Alan if he would mind if I brought them both round on their birthday for a brief guided tour, and as we had known each other for a large number of years he kindly said 'Yes'. Most successful people are very busy people and I had to organise this birthday treat six months in advance. I thought I should explain to my mum and dad that they couldn't rely on Alan being there as he was a busy man, but that we had the OK to look around the garden.

He treated them to a two-hour personal tour, including a lot of photographs and importantly one of Alan with his arms around them both. The highlight for them both was Alan himself making the tea and bringing them a tray of tea and biscuits. It was a memorable day and a birthday of a lifetime for them both. However, the story doesn't end there and I confess is somewhat emotive but, I feel, uplifting.

Unfortunately, some time later my dad had a very serious stroke and spent two months in the hospital rehabilitation ward. My dad was a very proud, independent and strong man, and initially he was extremely demotivated and demoralised with his incapacity. My mother cleverly took the picture into hospital of Alan Titchmarsh with arms around them both and placed it on his bedside cabinet. The nurses cunningly saw their opportunity and were always talking to my dad about the picture and teasing him about his celebrity contacts.

This strategy worked and this, allied with a burning desire to be back with his family, enabled him to slowly fight his way out of hospital to regain virtually 90 per cent of his previous capacity. Unfortunately, two years later my much-loved dad passed away, but my mum is convinced that the Alan Titchmarsh photograph started the change that gave all of our family two vital extra years.

Being rich can be challenging, honestly. The people at the Lotto operators Camelot conducted a MORI survey of past lottery winners. First, I should point out that only 4 per cent of Lotto winners were 'less happy' as a result of their wins and that 96 per cent were 'happier' or 'as happy' as before their good fortune. However, there are some surprising side-effects that come from winning the lottery: 40 per cent of Lotto winners admit to putting on weight after their win – obviously too many meals out; 55 per cent said the freedom to spend more time on hobbies was an important benefit – plenty of time then for marquetry; 21 per cent bought a caravan or camper van after winning – I would never have guessed this one; 66 per cent of the Lotto winners who gave up work reported that they missed their job; best of all is the reassuring fact that 76 per cent of Lotto winners said they gained more pleasure from giving than they did from spending. All winners over £250,000 are offered counselling and I think this is a good practice as, if caught, SWS (Sudden Wealth Syndrome) can be dangerous. On the other hand I'm sure we could all safely catch about £249,999 of it!

The world has known many famous people, most of whom have achieved their fame by extraordinary talent and in some cases genius, aided by perseverance, hard work and high levels of self-belief, often against all odds. Consider this historic list: Albert Einstein, William Shakespeare, Leonardo da Vinci, Elvis Presley, Walt Disney, Christopher Columbus, Mozart, Martin Luther King, Gandhi, Napoleon, Thomas Edison, Pele, John Lennon, Mohammad Ali, Isaac Newton, Mother Teresa, Madonna, Michael Jordan, Bobby Charlton, Tom Hanks, John Wayne, Queen Elizabeth I, Charles Dickens, Oprah Winfrey, Robin Williams, Bob Hope, Sean Connery, Paul Newman, W.G. Grace, Meryl Streep, Henry Ford, Jane Austen and, of course, Matt Le Tissier.

There are more uniquely modern ways of achieving fame that take less time, less talent (in fact no talent at all), less hard work and less perseverance. The following medley offers a range of choices for a fast-track to fame: having several huge boob jobs; filming yourself having sex; inheriting obscene amounts of wealth and rubbing people's noses in it; drinking, drug taking and partying like mad; marrying or dating a well-known sportsman and wearing nice clothes; being pretty and stopping eating (i.e. a supermodel); or just plain being a Royal.

The one key factor required for this modern fast-track to fame is the media and we are getting more and more of this, faster and faster. I once went on a 'Dealing with the Media' training course and the ex-journalist running the course very quickly destroyed any high-brow myths we had about the media by explaining that there is no such thing as 'good news' and no such thing as 'bad news', just 'news', so beware!

Because there are these fast-tracks to fame and then fortune, it has never been more obvious that the media creates a celebrity, often from being a 'nobody' to being famous just from being on TV, which brings us suitably to the next subject: reality TV.

10

I Don't Believe It!

Thus far we don't appear to have been blessed with a fly-on-the-wall documentary featuring Paris Hilton playing dominoes in her hotel room, but there is always hope. One has to say that reality TV is very popular and there is something strangely alluring about sitting at home on your settee, talking drivel and niggling at your couch-partner while you watch people on TV sitting on their settee, talking drivel and niggling with each other. I suspect it's reassuring to know this is reality, or not, as the case may be.

People seem to fall into two categories: those that absolutely love reality TV and those that hate it. In reality, whether we admit it or not, most of us regularly watch this genre of TV programme in one form or another. The more obvious reality shows such as *Big Brother* are of course probably the furthest from real life. For those who particularly dislike *Big Brother* their favourite pastime might be a game called 'Not watching reality TV' and this hobby may become even more popular across the country now we have been blessed with the headline 'Bucks Fizz to reunite and undergo group cosmetic surgery for a new reality TV show'.

The 'Not Watching reality TV' game requires a level of skill and dedication that is surprisingly challenging. Comfortably slouched on the settee, you start the game with the remote control in your right hand, ready to aim at the TV. You commence a normal evening's channel-hopping and you start to flick through the channels. The aim of the game is to spend as little time as possible watching reality TV during the allocated game time of two hours. The winner is the person who has still retained their sanity at 10 p.m. To achieve this, one has to be ready in an instant to click away from a channel if you inadvertently visit a reality TV programme. Even a small amount of reality time can lose you points. The strain on your right wrist and index finger can be intense. I know of someone who suffered a sudden cramp in their hand and before their wife returned to the room to rescue them, they tragically suffered five minutes of *America's Next Top Model*! I don't know of his final fate but we wish him well; a sad case indeed.

I have a particular wish to avoid cop reality shows as I am really uncomfortable watching car crashes, having suffered one myself and I am still suffering from a small degree of post-traumatic stress. As far as I can make out, the attraction of these shows is to watch in anticipation of being lucky enough to get a glimpse of a serious crime. Some cop reality programmes seem to specialise in affray, some in burglary and others drug overdoses. Some have a niche in petty car crime, but the worst of all for me are those that specialise in horrendous real-life car crashes.

On 13 March 2009 at 9.30 a.m. I performed some research on Sky TV to find out the extent of the challenges I would face in avoiding reality TV at that early hour of the day. I surveyed the first 76 channels and amazingly 37 programmes were a form of reality TV. No wonder some people's index fingers are sore, when over half of the content on TV offers some form of reality show. Of these 37 reality TV programmes, 21 were traditional reality shows, 3 were audience participation chat shows, 3 were quizzes and 10 were reality documentaries. The subject matter for the traditional reality shows was varied and fascinating; property improvement (5), motoring (2), air travel (2), weight loss (1), animals (3), ghosts (1), coach trips (1), antiques (1), gambling (1), car parking (1) and babies (3).

I found that of these 21 shows a number dealt with what I would consider to be some of the most tiresome of human experiences, with the two strangest being coach trips and parking your car. Without watching the programme it is hard to imagine the attraction of watching a group of ordinary people on a coach trip. Presumably the programme might excitingly include stops at motorway service stations, where people queue at cafés, occasionally the tea arrives cold, some of the group might take time-out to visit the toilets, the sign in the toilet might say that cleaning had taken place 1 hour and 45 minutes earlier, perhaps the coach driver stands outside and smokes a cigarette and, if you're really lucky, you can watch a child being sick on the coach! However, I haven't seen the programme and therefore I should withhold judgement, but I'm assuming this tale of ordinary life is underpinned by its lack of ordinary people on the coach and that changes everything.

I confess that I actually enjoy a number of reality TV shows, particularly the cookery programmes, and my wife is a big fan of forensic programmes, which seem to be one part reality TV and one part documentary. I have a concern that my wife's devotion to forensic programmes has led to her inadvertently gaining the knowledge necessary to commit the perfect murder. Of particular concern is my awareness of some recently recorded programmes *Forensic School* and, most worrying of all, *Women Who Kill Husbands*! Should our marriage take a dark turn, and I certainly don't expect or want this, then I could at least rest (although I hope not in peace or indeed in pieces) in the knowledge that I have broken her alibi for the perfect crime by publicly declaring my concerns.

The first reality TV programme appears to have been the 1948 show *Candid Camera* by Allen Funt and, for anti-reality TV people, his surname isn't a typing error. Following this, *You Asked for It* ran in the USA from 1950 to 1959, and this was the show where the audience first took part by voting on contestants. In 1964 Granada TV made a programme called *Seven Up* about 12 ordinary seven-year-olds with a view to making follow-up programmes every seven years. This was the first show in the country to make minor celebrities of ordinary people just because 'they were on the telly'.

In 1966 Andy Warhol made a short film called *Chelsea Girls* and we shouldn't be surprised that it took someone of his famed 'out-there' approach to help start the mayhem. Possibly the first reality TV programme that any baby boomers will remember is *The Family*, made in 1974 and featuring the Wilkins family of Reading. The next culprit came to us in 1976 and was wrapped up in a warm and comfy exterior and was a real wolf in sheep's clothing. The name of this Trojan horse of reality TV shows was *One Man and His Dog*, which was a programme about shepherds and their sheepdogs competing against each other in a far distant and wild place, being set strange challenges, with the winner taking all and complemented by a compelling Geordie voice-over, softly commentating on events. Does this sound familiar?

The Japanese took this up a notch or two when they started bizarre reality shows which ran through the 1980s and 1990s where the contestants had to perform strange, unpleasant and challenging tasks such as immersing themselves in a tank full of snakes. An example of such a show was *Gaki no Tsukai*, whose title isn't quite as catchy as *I'm a Celebrity Get Me Out Of Here*!

COPS came along in 1989, is still going strong and at the time of writing it has the traditional 'golden slot' of 8 p.m. on Saturday night FOX TV. The great thing about *COPS* is that there is an endless supply of potential future programmes. They probably started with *COPS New York* and then moved on to *COPS Los Angeles, Philadelphia, Dallas, San José, Chicago, Washington*; the list of opportunities is endless, with each venue offering the chance of some real criminal action.

However, in Britain one would assume the opportunities would be far less. Yes, historically we had the Gorbals in Glasgow, Moss Side in Manchester or any of the more dangerous areas of London, but I assumed that, beyond this, it was all a little tame compared to downtown LA. Of course I was completely wrong and I hadn't allowed for the modern British phenomenon of binge drinking. This popular pastime which is engaged in by many of today's younger citizens, now offers reality TV producers a myriad of opportunities for programmes about bad behaviour and we now have the likes of *Street Crimes, Booze Britain* and *Cops with Cameras*, including just the right amount of drunken brawling to both excite us and make us feel superior. When I saw a programme featuring the bad boys of Salisbury, I knew we had passed the point of no return. How long will it be before we get *Fighting in the Hamlets*, a popular reality programme about drunken brawling at village green cricket matches?

A Swedish show was made in 1997 called *Expedition Robinson*, which wasn't about the hunt to find a new barley water, but was in fact the forerunner to the most popular reality TV show of all time, *Survivor*. This programme, according to the *Guinness Book of Records*, gained the highest-ever reality TV rating. An incredible 51 million people or 41 per cent of the US viewing public watched the last programme in the series. The power of franchises being what they are, we of course have our own version of *Survivor* in the UK and we exported programmes such as *Pop Idol* to the USA, which became *American Idol*, plus many, many, many more.

Reality TV has become an industry in its own right, with a whole range of different types of programmes now being made. There seem to be 12 styles of programmes: the Documentary Fly-on-the-Wall (*The Family*), the Concocted Environment (*Big Brother*), Celebrities (*Katie and Peter*), Career Voyeurism (*COPS*), Elimination Shows (*The X Factor*), Dating (*Blind Date*), Hidden Hoax Camera (*Candid Camera*), Scaring People (*The Fear Factor*), Sports (*The Contender*), Make-over (*Fit Club*), Property (*A Place in the Sun*) and Social Experiments (*Wife Swap*).

This is the great thing about reality TV, the choice of subject matter is endless and you can get really specific as well. There is a programme entitled *Animal Cops Houston*, which excitingly seems to open the door for a potential new show called *Wife Swap Changing Rooms Bangkok*.

Appearing on a reality TV show must have mixed benefits. However, if you had a garden that looked like a tip and that was full of old prams and knee-high grass, then I can understand how coming back from a surprise weekend fishing with your brother-in-law, to find the charming Alan Titchmarsh, the buxom Charlie Dimmock and Tommy the minder-builder, at your home with champagne on ice and a nice new back garden crammed full of decking, sun loungers, pebbles and shrubs would be an extremely enjoyable experience. However, imagine the horrors of returning home to find your neighbours and Laurence Llewelyn-Bowen had turned your beloved lounge a deep purple colour with a sunken

Japanese pleasure pool. Still at least you would have been on the telly!

We were warned of all this and no one took any notice. In 1949 George Orwell published the classic book *Big Brother* in which he predicted that one day a TV programme of that name would be made that would appeal to the masses, gain enormous popularity, make ordinary people into celebrities and involve the audience watching and judging the protagonists' every move. As you probably know, this is not a true representation of the novel. The book actually predicts a future in which the State watches our every move from carefully positioned cameras, where life is brought down to its lowest common denominator and the masses get entertainment from watching people suffer. Thank goodness *that* didn't happen.

In George Orwell's book his lead character, Winston Smith, is taken into Room 101, which is a room in which people face their ultimate fear – in Winston's case his fear is rats. The TV producer people (sorry, the State Police) put a cage over Winston's head and threatened to let a starving rat into the cage unless Winston does what the producers (State Police) wanted. Bizarrely, we now have a TV programme called *Room 101* and it seems we really do create our own reality.

Ray Bradbury's book *Fahrenheit 451*, which was published in 1953, gave us a second clear warning regarding reality TV. In his book we live in a bookless society with wall-to-wall TVs that are two-way. The lead character's wife becomes involved in and is obsessive about an audience participation programme, which of course could never happen in real life. Just in case we missed both of these clear warnings the BBC ran a TV play in 1968 called The *Year of the Sex Olympics*, in which a dissident dictator is forced on to a remote island to keep the masses occupied via TV link; now there's a good idea.

All the signs were there; we simply ignored them and because of this we are faced with the prospect of a Room 101 of the future, where dissident TV viewers are placed in a padded room, without a

TV remote control and if they don't find a new form of barley water, they have to watch reality TV for 24 hours a day. Give me the rats anytime!

Straight after Brian had won £70,000 on *Big Brother* on 2 August 2001, the BBC website asked these two questions: 'Have programmes such as *Big Brother* and *Survivor* reached their peak?' and 'Will producers have to resort to even more outlandish gimmicks to keep viewers glued to their screens?' The answers are clearly, 'No' and 'Yes'; but some nine years later the end has come at last for *Big Brother* – for now!

For a few years I have sat on an idea for a new novel called *Reality Now*, which is a form of science fiction book that predicts the future through society's reality TV programmes, with a chapter for each developing new reality show every five years. The last show in 2060 would be called 'Survive to Live', in which all the players are convicted criminals and in which the losers, not to put too fine a point on it, are killed live on TV. The book would highlight the step-by-step lowering of the sensitivity bar as the producers resort to ever-more depraved activities to keep audience figures high. The key message would be that the slow step-by-step decline in society's morality wasn't noticed and that depravity became normality almost unnoticed. Incidentally, this is my own copyrighted idea and if a film producer is interested in making this idea into a film, please contact me – fast! Whatever we need to do or whatever you want changed, I will do it; anything to get this on the screen and whatever is necessary to get the audiences, let's do it. Oh dear, it seems my bar has already fallen.

To achieve a balanced view of reality TV I believe it's worth reminding ourselves of the stars that *Big Brother* has brought us; there is the late Jade Goody and well … no one else I can remember. I can understand the benefits of reality TV to ageing celebrities who are D Listed which actually means 'not really a celebrity at all'. These people are given the opportunity, though not without risk, to refresh their flailing careers and move up the league table to maybe the C or even the B List, normally just for a week or two. For some previously forgotten ex-celebrities, however, it has completely re-engineered their careers, losing them their 'ex' or in one case creating an 'ex'.

I can also appreciate the benefits to the TV production companies of this genre, as let's face it this is cheap (monetary) TV. How much can it cost to have a cameraman with a video recorder walk around someone's home for a couple of weeks? In theory, there are no props, no scripts, no make-up and no storyboard. Compare this to a production of one of those superb British dramas featuring David Jason that runs for two hours and includes some highly trained and skilled actors and actresses, an array of scriptwriters, make-up artists, producers, directors, researchers, stagehands, designers, costume people and many more. You certainly seem to get what you pay for in life.

Progress ensures we are already moving on past reality TV into a new form of reality media; this is of course YouTube, the online voyeurism site that allows you to watch a huge number of interesting, entertaining, historic and downright strange video clips that ordinary people download on to the site. It's free of course, but is definitely alluring, especially where you have a long-standing love such as 'Steam Train Runs of the 1950s', 'Joni Mitchell's 1971 World Tour' or 'Colchester United's Greatest Wins'.

The reality is that you will almost certainly find a classic clip of a long-lost love on YouTube and that's its attraction, as there is something for everyone. Ironically, we already have reality TV shows that show the best YouTube clips, which is, in essence, reality showing reality. In the future I wonder whether we will enjoy a classic reality TV show entitled *The 50 Best Reality Shows that Featured the YouTube Favourites?*

Here is another idea for a new reality TV show called *Celebrity Desert Island Sister Swap Fit Challenge*. The programme would involve pairs of carefully chosen, formerly famous sisters, who are stranded on a remote tropical island where their sibling rivalry comes to the fore in a bid to lose the most weight, while existing on a diet of only locusts. Just picture it, what a good idea!

I don't recall hearing of a recent government report that has found that reality TV is bad for your family well-being, but no doubt, sooner or later, we will be blessed with such a report, which brings us suitably to the next subject: home and families.

11

Home Sweet Home

The reality TV shows that feature families very often reflect a less than perfect family environment, examples being the 2009 version of *Wife Swap* and the original *The Family* from 1974 – some things never seem to change.

If we think of family and home, it's more than likely an image of a warm homely comfortable scene that comes to mind, because that is what home means for many of us and, if not a reality, then it's definitely a wish. Our home offers us escape from the rigours of the world and a place to luxuriate in the warmth of security and love. Modern society views the family as a form of haven from the world where intimacy, love, trust and protection are provided; well, that's the theory at least.

The United Nations Human Settlements Programme called 'Habitat' (which presumably plans to fill the world's houses with Swedish-style soft furnishings), estimates that 2 billion people or nearly one-third of the global urban population will be living in slums unless substantial changes are made. It seems we should definitely not take a roof over our head for granted.

A home is designed to provide us with many of life's core needs. Abraham Maslow's well-known hierarchy of physiological needs described in *A Theory of Human Motivation* in 1943 concludes that the following are the most basic human needs: breathing, food, water, sex, sleep, homeostasis and excretion. Let's explore how families do in fulfilling these seven basic human needs.

Breathing; well, even in the most dysfunctional families you rarely suffer strangulation and therefore, so far, so good. How do you feel we do with food? According to the National Statistics Office, on average males spend 1 hour 25 minutes a day eating and drinking and females some six minutes less. In my experience this isn't due to the fact that women gobble their food down more than men, it's because they don't seem to like food as much as men. Eating represents approximately 10 per cent of our waking day and therefore we clearly expend some significant time in fulfilling this basic need.

I have always enjoyed family mealtimes and there is a view held by many psychologists that the traditional family meal, sitting around the dinner table talking over the events of the day, has a strong bonding effect upon members of the family. It seems to have a primeval feel to it and it's like bringing home a warthog, fresh from the hunt, gutted, skinned and prepared by the woman of the family, roasting it over a hot fire in the cave and then the family talking about the adventures of the day. This is a long way from the often real family experiences of trays on laps, Sainsbury's ready-meals, sitting in front of the TV watching *The X Factor*.

The situation with water is equally encouraging as, in virtually all homes in the UK, cold fresh water is pumped into our homes ready to drink, bathe in, brush our teeth with, (if you are rich enough) swim in, water our flower beds, wash our cars, flush our little bombers away and, never to be forgotten, water down our malt scotch! It's seems to me that we take this resource of the modern Western world completely for granted and, if we were to live for any length of time in Africa's heartland or jump on a time machine back to Shakespearean England, running water would be the very first thing we would miss…well, perhaps just after TV.

In the Elizabethan age people didn't bathe throughout winter until spring. As summer finished they spread goose fat all over their bodies and sewed themselves into their undergarments, all sealed up until their spring-clean. Imagine the smell in March as all those sweaty bodies were unveiled. Even up until the 1800s water was precious and the officers on HMS *Victory* found it safer to provide their men with ale rather than putrid water. Let's face it, we ignore the importance of water at our peril – you often don't know what you have until you lose it.

Sex – yes please! Such is the primeval nature of this basic human need that we could easily fill the whole chapter with this emotive subject (we do have a chapter dedicated to sex and love later in the book). The National Statistics Office survey in 2005 researched how people in Britain spend their time and interestingly it doesn't include any time allocation for sex. For males we have 40 minutes dedicated to personal care, 23 minutes to reading, 37 minutes to hobbies and games, and 15 minutes to voluntary work, but nothing at all for sex! Unless the government is too shy to ask, the conclusion must be that sex for men involves such a small amount of time as to be too minute as to measure, or perhaps it's included in '13 Minutes Other'. Either way it is fascinating that an act that seems to be the be-all and end-all in our lives actually comes behind voluntary work in time input. Makes you think about the importance of giving, doesn't it?

Such is the importance of sleep to human beings that we have a whole chapter devoted to it later in the book. Needless to say, life is difficult if you can't get a good night's sleep. Isn't it true that there is very little in life as satisfying and reassuring as getting back into your own warm soft bed for eight hours of peaceful and blissful sleep? Imagine this, heaven. There is something about the familiarity, security and the predefined comfort of your own bed. It's akin to returning from a dangerous wild boar hunt in the woods to the safety and warmth of your cave and its fire – no wonder we call our home a castle.

Another of the other basic human needs is homeostasis, or more accurately human homeostasis, which is not the scientific term for a fear of Greek men dressed in leather, but actually 'the body's ability to regulate physiologically its inner environment to ensure its stability in response to external fluctuations', which is far less interesting than a fear of George Michael in his early breakthrough years.

Excretion is quite frankly a dirty business but at its best it's regular as clockwork. It's worth remembering that without excretion our bodies would quickly poison themselves and thus this daily cleanout has real physiological benefits. The next time my wife berates me for ruining the ambience and environment in our bathroom I will remind her that it is only by these actions that I can physiologically survive, or words to that effect. If one is honest, this daily or sometimes more frequent activity is a highly rewarding and, let's face it, an enjoyable experience. This needs to be said because I feel excretion gets a crap press and someone needs to speak up for it, before it gets washed away completely, so I have.

According to the Office of National Statistics in 2006 there were 17.1 million families, which was an increase over the preceding 10 years and this shows us that families can't be all bad. The ratio did move towards cohabiting couples as opposed to married couples and not unsurprisingly lone-parent families increased to almost one in seven of all families. In 2001 half of cohabiting couples were under the age of 35, which would suggest that they either moved on to marriage or ultimately split up; this would equate to a kind of seven-year returns policy: try it and see.

The sociologists refer to a conjugal family as a nuclear family, which means a family where the 'heads have sensual coupling' (strange phrase I know, but that's how sociologists describe it) or perhaps, in reality, one spark and the whole lot goes up! Despite this, we are still mainly traditionalists as 71 per cent of all families are headed by married couples and 90 per cent of dads go out to work. We have on average 1.8 children and half a pet per family, although this can vary from a pet python to a pet hamster, and I wouldn't recommend both in the same house other than as intended nutrition! Being children of the modern age, 40 per cent of us have two cars and Maggie Thatcher is probably proud to know that four out of five of us live in a mortgaged house. Not really a surprise is that 79 per cent of us have mobile phones and Bill Gates' 1980s vision of a PC in every home is only 65-per-cent true in the UK. You need to put in a bit more effort, Bill.

One interesting fact that was uncovered by Crédit Suisse is the relatively low percentage of family-owned businesses in the UK. We do much worse here than our European neighbours and the UK has the lowest proportion of family-owned businesses at 8 per cent of all businesses, whereas in Germany and France they have four times this number. However, this doesn't necessarily reflect a lack of entrepreneurial acumen, perhaps just the opposite, as it's tough enough to get on together in a family, let alone in business, and to confirm this, all you need to do is look at the Ewings of Dallas. Just one in six of UK family-owned businesses lasts three generations or more – it gets to them all!

As usual the politicians hijack anything that might be considered a good thing and it is widely believed that the nuclear family and its values is an essential ethical and cultural part of society. Most sound-thinking people would agree with this but isn't it fun how the politicians jump on to the bandwagon and then fall flat on their faces? John Major's government proudly promoted their support of family values, only subsequently to be undermined by the breaking news story of his affair with Edwina Currie. Considering Edwina's preachy style on subjects such as eating eggs and John's on family values, these revelations were somewhat ironic. I have to admit I quite liked them both, but this sorry tale just highlights the dangers of preaching; I told you so.

As a politician you have to keep your own house (or two) in order and for most of us this is still mainly tasked to women, who, according to the National Statistics Office in 2005, on average spent 3 hours a week doing housework, whereas men input a paltry 1 hour 41 minutes. The biggest female commitment to the household chores is ironing, for which a staggering 11 out of 12 women are responsible. There is a strong argument to include ironing in the school curriculum as of course we already have both boys and girls catered for with DIY, so why not ironing? Just an idea. I know this isn't very PC but it's exceedingly practical.

More support, however, to the conclusion that males are becoming modern men is the news that at the weekend male housework input rises by approximately 40 per cent and so you see, ladies, nagging does work! Men do often get a raw deal from their lady partners in life, although it has to be said that there is some evidence to suggest they do deserve it. Imagine a young child; she has momentarily lost her dad in a shopping centre and is found wandering by a security guard who needs to help her urgently find her protector and mentor in life. The security guard asks the child, 'What's your dad like?' and sadly, probably in many cases, the answer would be, 'Beer and football' ... from the mouth of babes! Perhaps women do have a point.

Men and women are so different, aren't they? A friend of mine told me of an occasion when his son was young and his wife was passing the baby's room and just caught a glimpse of my friend longingly looking down at his son's cot as he slept. With a tear in her eye she snuggled up to him and whispered lovingly into his ear, 'Penny for your thoughts?' His automatic reply didn't enhance his immediate love life; 'Do we have the warranty on this crib? Those slats aren't straight.' Sometimes you just can't win.

At the risk of stating the blindingly obvious, choosing to have children is a very big decision. For most people, children come with a lifetime's burning desire to nurture and love, in parallel with a serious sense of responsibility. We can attend training courses for dog handling, advanced driving, archery, sub-aqua diving and, of course, marquetry but only recently have we been blessed with courses on parenting and of course *Super Nanny*. The best parenting advice I could find was Jeremy Kyle's on his TV programme where he groups together the most irresponsible and worst of Britain's parents so that he can yell at them to tell them not to be angry. He also suggests how they might do it better, although quite frankly any way would be better than the kind of thing you see on his show.

When your children are small, life is fairly simple with cute daughters all dressed up in frocks and boys with whom you can enjoy a football kick-around. You get lulled into a false sense of euphoria because, when you are least suspecting it, up creeps the horror of all horrors for parents, those teenage years. Your little girl suddenly turns into the most unreasonable and selfish female on earth and your sweet little boy gets attitude. They move in a flash from wanting you to provide for their every need, to being embarrassed to be seen in public with you. How did you go from being the cornerstone of their life and their provider, to a pariah, in the blink of an eye?

I sometimes wonder whether businesses should go on a recruitment drive to employ teenagers – to get them while they still know it all! However, like all things, this phase passes and before you know it they are enriching your life again by providing you with grandchildren and wondrously you actually become nostalgic about their teenage years, which is reframing at its best.

If you have more than one child then you probably have to deal with sibling rivalry. I was reminded of this dynamic when at a recent family event my eldest daughter was delighted to remind me, at least with a friendly laugh, that she had fewer dental fillings than her brother. Bearing in mind she is a grown woman with children of her own, we both saw the funny side of this, although it's clear that sibling rivalry seems fairly powerful, long-lasting and has teeth.

The sociologists say that this is a good thing as it teaches children conflict resolution and, because life is full of stress and challenges, it teaches us diplomacy and reasoning skills. They argue that sibling rivalry teaches children that the world isn't fair. I will second that and, now I know that sibling rivalry is a sign of a healthy family, my life is getting fairer by the minute.

Unfortunately, there is a darker side to some families and the 2001 Criminal Statistics found that on average 42 per cent of female murder victims are killed by current or former partners and therefore it's no wonder the police are so suspicious of partners in murder investigations. I will take this opportunity to just remind my wife that, should she be planning the perfect murder, not only is her cover already blown (see Chapter 10), but the police will know there is a 42-per-cent chance she did it anyway!

Children need extra protection and the NSPCC does a great job in trying to protect vulnerable children. The old tale that we care more about animals than children, because we have the Royal Society for the Protection of Animals and the National Society for the Prevention of Cruelty to Children just isn't true as the NSPCC was incorporated by Royal Charter in 1895.

Despite all these black statistics, a BBC poll in 2007 found some surprising but extremely encouraging results about how we feel in the UK regarding our families. A massive 93 per cent of us described our family life as 'fairly happy or very happy'. There is even some financial encouragement, as a couple without children spend £263.60 per person per week and yet a household with children reduce this to £155.60 per person per week and so there is economic leverage in a family.

However, best of all, the BBC found that when asked who are you happiest with, which is in fact the ultimate question, 6 per cent said 'on my own', 2 per cent said 'with work colleagues', 17 per cent said 'with friends', 2 per cent said 'don't know' (avoid these people) and a huge majority of 73 per cent said, yes, you guessed it, 'my family'. Strangely seven out of ten people feel family life is becoming less successful and yet 73 per cent are happiest with their own family. We clearly value family life and understand its importance, and thus our concerns, and isn't that just reassuring and heartwarming?

Not only that, but there is scientific research to confirm the value of a marriage. In a study run by the Karolinsha Institute in Sweden over two decades and published online by the *British Medical Journal* it was shown that divorcees and widows faced three times the risk of Alzheimer's disease later in life. You see, if you are married it's keeping you and your spouse healthy. You need to remember this!

The heart of the home still rests with cohabiting couples and, lest we forget, one of the areas that gives most joy – and, perversely, friction – is the physical coupling of the heads of the household, which brings us suitably to the next subject: love and sex.

12

You Sexy Thing

One woman who can't enjoy both sex and home life together, well at least not noisily and legally, is a 48-year-old lady from Washington on Wearside, who in April 2009 was given a four-year ASBO, banning her from making excessive noise anywhere in England. Neighbours had complained to police about early-morning noises including shouting, groaning and the banging of the bed against the wall. They say love makes the world go round and, even if it doesn't quite do this, it certainly keeps things interesting. One thing is for sure and that is without love and sex the human race would become extinct.

'You Sexy Thing' was a pop song recorded by Hot Chocolate and written by Errol Brown. It reached number two in the UK singles charts in 1975 and also number three in the US charts. It is the only song to enter the UK charts in three successive decades, 1970s, 1980s and 1990s, and as it started its life as a lowly B-side, it just shows there is always hope for love and sex and maybe all you need to do to hit the top is turn over. When the song was written there were some thoughts that it might be banned because its lyrics were then considered frank. This really does highlight the paranoia that our society has about love and its physical outpourings: on the one hand intrigued and seduced and on the other potentially outraged and perhaps ashamed. 'Oh you are naughty, but I like you.'

We are fairly unique amongst the animal kingdom in that we participate in sexual intercourse even when the female is not in oestrus, which means we do it for pleasure, not just procreation. We share this privilege with dolphins and chimpanzees, which is perhaps why we feel such kindred to these two species.

In fact, surprisingly scientists confirm that sex has a number of significant health benefits. These benefits include fighting off illness as sex apparently helps ward off disease. According to Dr Carl Charnetski of Wilkes University having one or two sexual episodes a week boosts the immune system – no wonder you feel good afterwards! It also wards off depression, as a study by Dr Gordon Gallup of the State University of Albany found that women who regularly engaged in sex were significantly less depressed than those who were not as regular. I knew it!

Sex helps holds back the ageing process because it helps you look younger, as a study by Dr David Weeks of Royal Edinburgh Hospital reported that men and women who had sex on average four times a week looked approximately ten years younger than they really were. A more cynical interpretation might be that there may be a chance that people who look younger than they really are, have more chance of more sex, but this is just a random thought.

Not to ignore losing weight, because sex burns calories at 300 an hour. You can do the maths yourself – that's at least ten calories a go! With all this scientific data I intend to prepare a detailed proposal paper for my wife, outlining the overwhelming scientific evidence for us to upgrade our well-being programme, or on second thoughts, maybe not.

Unfortunately, this would be unlikely to succeed because no doubt she would remind me that men focus too much on the physical and not enough on romance. This looks like it's true in Wales, as when Wrexham bus company Arriva Wales offered a complete Valentine's Day experience in a personalised 'Will you marry me?' bus, complete with chocolates, champagne, cherubs, hearts and harps, not one man took it up. Maybe if they tried this in a leap year, it might just work.

Further evidence of this male romantic reticence comes from the BBC with the news that in 2006 a Jersey dating club, the *After 8 Club*, was suffering from a shortage of men. This is somewhat puzzling, as I would have thought this type of organisation was exactly what single men wanted. However, I think I might have found the answer to this Channel Islands mystery. A study by Dr Thomas Pollett of Newcastle University suggests that rich men give their partners more orgasms and this is yet another reason to be envious of them. Given that Jersey is full of rich men, or at least according to *Bergerac* it is, then my theory is that these wealthy super-lovers just don't need to go to dating clubs to get hitched up.

Maybe, just maybe, it might be the money that's the attraction for women to lie when surveyed about their rich sugar daddy's prowess in bed, although possibly my objectivity is waning here as envy rises to the surface.

At the time of writing we are in a recession and perversely this provides our love lives with fresh hope. A YouGov survey of 20,000 British adults found sex was the most popular low-cost activity and, unlike many goods and services in the recession, sex toy sales are booming. What this probably means is that we turn to love, companionship, comfort and, dare I say, excitement when we feel insecure, and why not?

Unfortunately, sex isn't always safe though. Sexually transmitted diseases, or STDs, are on the increase; or rather more precisely the number of people suffering from them is on the increase. Young people represent approximately 12 per cent of the population, although they account for nearly half of all those diagnosed with sexually transmitted diseases. I assume you can rule out those over 75 and you should be able to rule out those under 16, but this is still a large percentage. STDs all appear so awful and even the very sound of their names seems to be redolent of their horrors: syphilis, gonorrhoea, chlamydia, herpes, genital warts, crabs and bacterial vaginosis. They sound and, I'm sure, *are* horrendous. You wouldn't want any of these, would you?

HIV is obviously the most dangerous of STDs and there are 25 different types of sexually transmitted diseases which are treated at Genitourinary Medicine Units, or GUMs. However, despite this wholly inappropriate three-letter acronym, these clinics do a great job. In the year 2007 these GUMs diagnosed 397,990 cases and I suspect too much wine has often led to the lack of caution which in turn led to the visit to the GUM. Which suggests less WINE would mean less GUMs.

With such a problem for modern society it's important that our young people are educated in the ways of sex and a report from Sir Alasdair Macdonald has examined how personal, social and health education should become part of the school curriculum in England. It would mean very young children from age 5 to 16 learning about life skills including sex, healthy eating and money. From the age of 7, children would learn about puberty, which might be a touch zealous, as I doubt many kids hit this wall until at least 11. Although this report caused quite a stir, with headlines such as 'Sex Education for 5-Year-olds', there might be a few parents breathing a sigh of relief.

Telling your children about sex has to be one of the more challenging of your tasks as a parent. I remember my dad giving me a book and saying, 'This should tell you everything you need to know.' I dread to think what story my son would give of my incompetent efforts at parental sex education. You get the distinct feeling that you are more embarrassed than they are, don't you? I remember avidly sitting through those awful sex education films at school but in those days we didn't have *Men and Motors* or *Bravo*, so for a 13-year-old boy you had to take what titivation you could get!

Isn't it amusing that as a young adult sex is both frightening and captivating, strangely both at the same time? No wonder some of us grow up with hang-ups. As a young boy it's difficult enough learning about how the body works, without having to worry about what females need and that, when you become sexually active (with a separate breathing human being that is), you also need to perform.

Despite all our modern openness, frankness and apparent compulsion towards sex, in 2003 the Kinsey Institute found that women today now have less sex than their 1950s counterparts. It seems the male chauvinistic image of a 1950s stay-at-home mum, keeping a nice tidy house, cooking a meal full of fresh vegetables, slippers ready at the door, sat waiting for her man to return from the office, is nearer to reality than would be expected. However, if society makes women work full-time in employment and expects them to be homemakers as well, then it's not a great surprise to find that the negligee gets left in the bottom of the drawer.

Another interesting piece of information the Kinsey Institute found in their survey of just under 1,000 women was that single women who cohabit with male partners are 27 per cent more likely to have sex two or three times a week than married women. I assume this also means married women are 27 per cent more likely to have the traditional headache.

In reality all of our lives today are so filled by our jobs, responsibilities, raising children, watching TV and, if we have any time left over, going to the gym, it is little wonder sex takes a bit of a back seat. This is perhaps further evidenced by a report on the BBC about the World Congress of Sexology held in Paris back in 2001 on ladies aged over 50. Our French, Swiss and German counterparts apparently enjoy approximately twice as much sex as British women. Despite this, two-thirds of British women felt it was very important for them to maintain a satisfying sex life, but this was in 2001!

This just seems to confirm that the more hectic and intense a life we lead, the more likely there will be an effect upon our natural desires, and it looks like women are right and love and sex are intrinsically entwined. A BBC News headline read: 'Cuddles more important than sex.' They also reported a survey by redirect.co.uk which found that, seven years into their relationship, a massive four out of five of women said they still found their partner attractive, so no evidence at all for the seven-year itch. Phew! However, half of the women surveyed said they wanted their men to be more romantic and here is the problem for men, how? There are 12 million unattached people in Britain and for us attached men to avoid joining this group, we had better become romantic. But what do we need to do?

Here is the problem that men face. Women love their feelings, are comfortable with them and luxuriate in them. How do you deliver a feeling, when as a man you are physiologically conditioned to seek out problems and solve them? If you solve a woman's problem you effectively steal her emotion, which is not good when you are trying to be romantic. This is probably why women, when asked for examples of desired romantic behaviour from men, mention such simple things as cosy meals in, walks in the countryside, breakfast in bed and being made a cup of tea. No wonder ladies get frustrated with men as this stuff is pretty basic, isn't it?

With all this pressure on men to deliver the goods, it is little wonder that they had to invent sildenafil citrate. The more recognised term for Pfizer's sildenafil is the trade name Viagra, although there are now many competitors to Viagra which is well on its way to becoming the Hoover of erectile enhancement, in a branded way of course! This erectile dysfunction drug was first available from 1998 and although you may not be aware of it, is in fact another of those great British inventions. If you currently take these tablets, next time you partake, wouldn't it be appropriate and respectful to take time out to think of Queen and country and please be proud to stand up for the nation! Sildenafil was first synthesised in Sandwich in Kent and the first clinical trials were in Swansea. The imagination runs wild with the thought of the clinical trials for Viagra. How did they *measure* success with these trials? The drug has obviously offered healthy mature men a chance to extend their love life, which wouldn't otherwise have been available and this must be a good thing.

I understand that one of the problems with taking the drug is that one has to time things, well, let's say, just right. Imagine if one took a tablet in anticipation of some cuddling with one's wife, probably immediately after a walk in the country, followed by a romantic meal and then a cup of tea, but just as things had started to inevitably progress the family popped in, unannounced. This would be somewhat embarrassing. I wonder how many hours it would be before one could socialise in a civilised way. Viagra seems like an Exocet missile because once it's on its way and on target there's no stopping it.

Most of us have heard of Viagra's erectile effects but you may not be aware that it has been reported to have other less obvious uses. Sildenafil is reported to help with altitude sickness and the treatment of high-altitude pulmonary oedema, which would be particularly beneficial to mountaineers. They say men think of sex every two minutes and climbing mountains must be difficult enough without the added challenge of having to avoid those 30-times-an-hour amorous thoughts just to keep clear of all those jagged edges.

The 2007 Ig Nobel Prize in Aviation (a parody of the real Nobel Prizes) went to Patricia V. Agostino, Santiago A. Plano and Diego A. Golombek of the National University of Quilmes in Argentina for their discovery that Viagra aids jet lag recovery in hamsters. They found that hamsters recovered twice as fast when on Viagra. This was found only to work when the hamsters travelled in an easterly direction. Therefore, if you have a randy pet rodent that needs to get from Buenos Aires to London in a hurry, you now have just the solution. Science is a wonderful thing, isn't it?

The South Americans also seem to have taken Viagra's use to a new height with further news that a Bolivian football team's physiotherapist mixed Viagra with the team's half-time fruit juice to help them play at high altitude, although the makers of the drug make it clear it should be used only as prescribed. Asked about the effects upon the team's performance, Mr Figueroa said, 'At altitude you win, you draw, you lose. The best results came when the team relied upon strong tactical nous'; and so it seems that, as in life, as in love, working together in tandem scores every time.

Viagra's emergence highlights humanity's obsession with sex and when researching this chapter on the Internet, our obsession became very apparent. I had to be particularly careful regarding which keywords to enter in my search engine. If you inadvertently type in a word such as 'adult' you get literally millions of results and at the top of the search are typically the coarsest sites. 'Adult education' has a different meaning on the Internet, as it doesn't mean a course on marquetry at the local technology college! Now we are in the digital worldwide Internet era, we really do need new laws to regulate and manage society's morality as the Obscene Publications

Act was enacted in 1857 at the height of Victorian prudery and, let's face it, things have changed.

If you have travelled to Amsterdam you have probably walked around the Red Light District, for no other reason than your inquisitiveness as a curious tourist. When my wife and I visited Amsterdam we spent one early-summer evening strolling hand-in-hand (for my protection) through the said district. What a bizarre and strangely disconcerting experience this was! To see sex marketed so openly just like any other product and, in fact, better than most products.

While in Amsterdam we hired some bicycles and cycled around the city to enjoy the beautiful sites. Amsterdam is full of cyclists and when you cross the road it is the cyclists, not the motorists, you have to watch out for. This is quite a change from here in the Britain, which brings us suitably to the next subject: transport and motoring.

13

They Drive Me Mad

The Netherlands is a very flat country and I'm sure cycling around the Dutch countryside is considerably more enjoyable than cycling through Central London. This is despite former mayor Ken Livingstone's efforts with the Congestion Zone. For those not familiar with the Central London Congestion Zone, it is highlighted by a big red C displayed on road signs at its perimeter. When you encounter this it feels like an invisible *Star Trek*-style force field protecting our nation's capital – 'Get the shield back up, Scotty.'

On one particular day I was driving to a hotel on the very edge of the Congestion Zone and had to avoid entering the Big Red C to ensure I didn't incur a fine. The road to the hotel I was visiting skirted the no-go zone, and I played a cat-and-mouse game which involved teasing the Big Red C as at one moment I appeared to be going straight into the zone but somehow at the last minute raced off to the right or left to skim along its perimeter. I have to admit this was somewhat invigorating and when you do avoid the Big Red C you feel a strong sense of achievement. I'm not sure this was the kind of reaction the road traffic planners intended.

Despite this, the excess of motoring in our country has to stop somewhere, as the motor car seems to be inexorably taking over our cities, towns and villages. According to the Ordinance Survey we have 2,705 miles of motorways in the UK, 29,934 miles of A roads, 18,779 miles of B roads and an incredible 195,395 miles of minor public roads. This compares to a paltry 173 miles of pedestrianised streets and yet there still aren't enough roads.

People used to talk about 'going for a nice quiet Sunday afternoon drive', but this is just not possible anymore. Sundays are now often busier on the roads than weekdays, with all of us rushing around to get to Homebase, B&Q, the local garden centre, watching sporting events, a fun day at the shopping mall or going to the mother-in-law's for lunch. There is no escape from motor vehicles and you can see why, because according to the National Statistics Office between 1971 and 2007 the proportion of households with a car increased from 52 per cent to 75 per cent. Indeed in the same period the number of households with two cars increased more than fourfold. When you include foreign visitors, UK roads are clogged up by almost 33 million vehicles a year, but I'm guessing you didn't need me to tell you that.

Given that motor cars are clearly so popular, it's interesting that such groundbreaking technology took so long to be fully exploited. The first automobile patent was granted in 1789 and fuel gas-powered internal combustion engines first appeared as long ago as 1806. It wasn't until 1885 that a petroleum-fuelled internal combustion engine appeared which was built by Karl Benz, the grandfather, of course, of Mercedes Benz. Peugeot was formed in 1891 and by the start of the twentieth century the automotive industry was beginning to gain momentum.

Normally it's we British who have a great idea but then let others take over and make the real money from it, as with our nation's great computer mishap. However, when it comes to motor vehicles, it's the French who missed the boat. In 1903 French motor car production was 30,204 cars, which was an incredible 49 per cent of worldwide production. Today 49 per cent of the market would represent approximately 20 million cars which would now be made each year in France. This would mean it would be fairly easy to get a job in Sauhaux, the largest industrialised site in France. The more relevant question is: Could Jeremy Clarkson have tolerated 20 million Citroëns and Renaults being built every year?

In Britain we didn't help our commercial cause by the passing of the Locomotive Act in 1865, famously requiring self-propelled vehicles on public roads to be preceded by a man on foot waving a red flag and honking a horn. The law was not repealed until 1896 and its original passing must have been met with glee in Paris. Needless to say the Americans eventually took over this great business opportunity and the first car produced for the masses was the Oldsmobile. Business boomed and between 1904 and 1908 there were 241 brand-new car production companies formed in the US and one of these was the Ford Motor Company. Henry Ford introduced innovative and affordable pricing, as well as mass-production techniques, and the rest is history.

He may not realise this, but 23 July 1904 changed David Beckham's life as this was the day in history that Ford sold its first car. I think everyone remembers their very first car, possibly because it almost certainly took such financial sacrifice to acquire your first wheels! David Beckham's first car was a Ford Escort, although today, if he chooses of course, he can afford a Rolls-Royce Silver Phantom whose upholstery uses 15 hides of leather.

My own first car was a Triumph Herald Estate. This cost me £200, which at that time was a lot of money, representing for me four months' wages. I bought it from a neighbour and it was – and there is no other way of saying this – a horrible car. Whenever we had cold weather I had to allow at least 30 minutes to spray WD-40 all over the working parts to carefully tease, tickle and nurture it into life, and when I eventually did get it going, you needed to be a weightlifter to change gear. The doors didn't close properly either, so you always had plenty of natural ventilation. This was enhanced by a rather cute hole in the floor that displayed the tarmac as you drove along! Because of all this internal airflow, whenever it was below zero degrees outside, ice would form inside the car.

After a very traumatic and troubled relationship, we parted company in almost tragic circumstances. While driving along at 50 miles an hour on my way to work one day, the car decided to sit down on the road and give up. The suspension gave way, as did the wheels, and I ended up travelling 100 yards on the tarmac with sparks flying everywhere. We parted company reasonably amicably, it to a scrapyard and me to a second-hand car dealer to buy a proper car. You may have more generous and fond memories of your first car, but whether you do or not, I'm sure you remember what make it was, its colour and what it cost you. Is this correct?

Motor cars need people to drive them and it seems that we fall into several types of motor beings. The two extremes of these motor beings highlight the highly emotive nature of driving. The first of these might be called 'Not Sures'. These people are very unsure about the whole concept of driving and especially the technological side: 'What happens if I break down?' 'Not Sures' don't enjoy driving one little bit and they do their very best not to draw too much attention to themselves on the road and just about timidly get from A to B without too much trauma. However, this badly backfires when they create a nice half-mile procession behind them when they crawl along a country road at 25 miles an hour.

The completely opposite type of driver to a 'Not Sure' is what we might call, quite simply, a 'Car Lover'. If you are one of this group you are likely to love motor vehicles, take a passionate interest in your own car, as well as everyone else's cars, always aspire to own a better car, meticulously look after your own, talk a lot about cars, think a lot about cars and often drive very fast. These are the group who subscribe to car magazines and who stand in the hangar as the audience on *Top Gear*.

The two extremes of Not Sures and Car Lovers pretty much can't engage together in any form of meaningful conversation about cars – one speaks Swahili and the other Chinese. Not Sures will never become road-rage antagonists but are perfectly set up to be victims of road rage and as a result we all live together on the roads in perfect harmony – amen!

Whatever type of motor being you are, it's true we do change our personalities when we get behind the wheel. Do you remember the Walt Disney character Goofy who changed from a mild-mannered and friendly individual to a demon who charged everyone off the road the instant he got behind the wheel? I used the term 'individual' because I'm not quite sure what Goofy is; could he be a mix of dog and cow, or is he a dog with a horse's teeth? However, we digress.

Disney's cartoon character very cleverly highlighted the amazing Incredible Hulk-style transformation that overtakes drivers once they get behind the wheel. Road rage is becoming a major social problem and we already have a number of horrendous examples of murders, provoked by such a heinous crime as the victim cutting the killer up at a road junction. How could any human being so lose perspective as to murder or maim another person just because they slightly inconvenienced them on a motorway? We won't defend under-taking but surely let the punishment fit the crime?

A Gallup poll in 2003 showed that at some time 80 per cent of drivers have been a victim of road rage and this figure isn't coming down. More worrying was a *Max Power* study of their readers between 16 and 30 years old which found that 70 per cent admitted to committing road rage and of those who committed this offence a staggering 60 per cent said they did not regret it at all, as their victims 'deserved what they got'.

The most common expression of road rage is gesticulating and I'm sure when they say this they don't mean a friendly wave, but gesticulating rudely, probably *very* rudely. Why would people offer such coarse hand signs to fellow citizens that they wouldn't dream of delivering on the street? Of course it doesn't just stop at gesticulation and the US Automobile Association website has horrendous stories that include this quote from an offender: 'He was playing the radio too loud, so I shot him.'

It is very odd that these completely irrational surges of anger and emotion are brought on by such innocuous actions of fellow road users as tailgating, cutting-up, not saying thank you when being let in, driving with fog lights on when it's not foggy, under-taking, pulling out from a road junction making us slow down fractionally, getting in the wrong lane because they don't know the road layout like we do, not driving at least 80 miles an hour, stealing our car parking space … basically just inadvertently being there.

How would we respond if we were walking along a street and someone walked past us on the inside of the pavement? Would we race after them and then jump in front of them, almost knocking them over? If someone inadvertently walked in front of us from a side street and we had loads of time to avoid walking into them, but we had to just slow our pace a little, would we mouth an obscenity at them? If we were walking around a shopping mall and we saw a nice seat to rest our feet on for a minute or two and someone didn't see us but got to the seat before us, would we wildly gesticulate at them and race off in anger to find another seat? No doubt the answer is 'no' to every question, because, if not, people would lock us up for being slightly insane, wouldn't they? On the road though, it's standard practice.

In a reversal of our 'deferred success' (see Chapter 7) with the invention of the computer, the Americans invented road rage and in Britain we have taken this invention and really run with it. The term 'road rage' seems to have started when in 1988 the *St Petersburg Times* in Florida reported: 'A fit of road rage has landed a man in jail, and accused of shooting a woman passenger whose car had cut him off on the highway.' It has got so bad that lollipop wardens in Wrexham have even had to learn self-defence to defuse any possible road rage confrontations. What is it all coming to?

If you want to get back at all those angry motorists, but in a non-aggressive and more subtle way, then there are three things you might imagine but please don't actually do them. When sat alone in your car and stopped at some traffic lights, try having an animated conversation with a phantom passenger sitting next to you – that will worry them! Alternatively, when stopped at a red light in one of two lanes, cast a glance at the motorist parallel with you and immediately, highly visibly and in a fearful state, make a big show of locking your doors for safety. Finally, you might cut out letters from a newspaper, stick them on some white card, in the style of kidnappers, and then Sellotape this to your back window, just like those cute car stickers: '**H E L P   M E   P L E A S E! I   A M   A   B A D   D R I V E R.**' That should do it! Unfortunately, all this is likely to do is to attract attention to you and probably the wrong type of attention, which is why I say: **D O N'T   A C T U A L L Y   D O I T**!

Why do people behave in such an appalling way and in fact in a manner they probably wouldn't dream of repeating away from the wheel? Studies have shown that as drivers we consistently overestimate our own driving skills and ability, which in turn feeds our belief that other drivers are not as able as ourselves. Therefore, the problem with road rage appears to be our over-egged ego, so not much of a surprise there.

This explains only why we create these situations; it doesn't explain why we behave so inappropriately. Modern motor vehicles, unlike my old Triumph Herald Estate with its natural air conditioning, create a cocooned environment of a private, near-indestructible space that is ours and only ours. First, we will not tolerate others entering this private space, and, second, we feel safe enough to project the kind of hostility we wouldn't feel able to do away from our cocooned driver's seat. Given that, when driving both parties are operating in this isolated environment, it is little wonder events escalate out of control ... and Goofy rules.

Modern cars include an array of gadgets and high-tech tools to make our journeys that much more comfortable. They include hi-fi systems that would out-blast a Led Zeppelin 1972 concert amplifier system. If this weren't enough we have air conditioning, digital clocks, traffic warning interruptions on the radio, fuel consumption readings, cruise control, guides where the nearest petrol stations are and warnings about speed controls. Overall, in today's vehicles we have more computing power than was used on Apollo 11. That got three men to the Moon and back, which, lest you have forgotten, is considerably further than Milton Keynes.

Like so much of modern life, driving is now a cocooned and high-tech experience. This vehicular technology is all very well but do you ever use it all? I don't. Cruise control is completely useless on Britain's overcrowded roads. If you put your car on cruise control, at let's say 84 miles per hour (to be slightly risqué), you are constantly breaking or accelerating to avoid the lane congestion, which of course negates the major benefit of cruise control. Get on a long straight American interstate highway, now that's a different matter: put your feet up, have a picnic, and just relax.

Motor vehicles, just like trains in Chapter 4, are inanimate objects; in other words they do not move or exist without a human being in control. We don't seem to like this reality very much as many of us make every attempt we can to humanise our cars. Some people give them names, others sex them (male or female) and of course we make movies about them: Herbie had feelings, was male and a real-life Disney character.

Could it be that we see our car as an extension of ourselves and a form of outer metallic ego? If so, this would explain many of the more bizarre behaviours which arise when cars and people mix. Automobile manufacturers have worked all this out for themselves, which is why they sell cars using large doses of sex, machismo and emotion. Some *undertake* surveys to find out what is the sexiest car, which doesn't mean the car you would most like to have sex in, but refers to the car that's the sexiest, that's owned by a person and thus who you would most like to have sex with!

The car owned by women that most turns men's heads, at least according to Evescar.com, is the Mercedes SL Roadster, famously driven by Grace Kelly in *High Society*, Can it be a coincidence that it's popular and driven by a beautiful women? I think not. The car is described as a mix of modern, high-performance, refined, classy and old-school, which sounds verging on schizophrenic. Alex Jenner-Fust, editor of Evecars.com, commented, 'The vintage Mercedes SL Roadster is undeniably a beautiful car, which oozes style and class. Buying one isn't cheap, but it proves the owner appreciates the finer things in life.' A possible conclusion from this might be that men like their women; attractive, well-groomed, sophisticated, expensive to maintain, hungry for life, mature, but still looking young. Don't men just want their cake and eat it?

If all you owned was a 12-year-old, young David Beckham-style Ford Escort, at least you had a chance to change it when the government of the day encouraged you to swap it in for a more economical, up-to-date and cost-effective model. If you didn't take up their bounty, you lost your chance but will this set a precedent for all ageing machines and will something similar follow for husbands? This could be dangerous. If this were to happen, I can only hope that my wife is satisfied with her old battle-scarred vintage Jag, which, if you get it out on a Sunday for a little relaxed drive, can still get up to 70 mph for a few minutes, but only if you change gear carefully. Still at least the seats are real leather and the dashboard is wood, albeit a little faded now.

The battle of the sexes continues to rage on the roads and in today's world of equality woman compete on a level playing field with men at road rage, speeding, bad driving, car-talk and most motoring things but, interestingly, not navigation, as you will notice they never talk about journey routes. You rarely hear a woman getting excited about discussing the latest roadworks on the A303; it's always men.

However, when men and women are in a car together the friction elevates to a new level. Progress means we now have satnav to replace road maps, just so you can now argue with your spouse, not, as in the past over her map-reading skills, but whether the satnav should be obeyed or not, but more on this later.

Despite all this equality, some motoring basics haven't changed and the big question still remains, 'Where are all the women Formula 1 drivers?' The answer is that there aren't any at all and in fact during the whole history of Formula 1 racing the total number of points won by the fairer sex is half a point. In the 1975 Spanish Grand Prix Leila Lombardi gained one point, which was later reduced to half a point because the race was not completed. Sorry, ladies, this is a fact, not sexist prejudice, and isn't it time this changed?

According to *AutoTrader* the fastest ever production car was the SSC Ultimate Aero which had a top speed of 257 mph. This is typical of today's production cars which can go at almost double the UK maximum speed limit, but why? Unless you break the law, risk other drivers' lives and lose your licence, you can never use all this spare speed. I can understand the need for acceleration, but why all this wasted horsepower? Is it simply because we can? We love speed, don't we, and thus the popularity of Formula 1 motor racing, car chase films like *Bullitt*, TV shows like *Top Gear* and *Police Camera Action*. This investment in speed is no better exemplified than by *AutoTrader*'s top 100 motoring trivia that included the fact that apparently McLaren's engine bay was gold-plated because it reflects the heat best. Boys and their toys, eh!

If you do have a nice car it does elicit a degree of envy, and *poor* Wayne Rooney suffered this when his car was maliciously damaged while parked in May 2006. This appears a uniquely British trait as it seems in the United States even the poorest people respect and admire successful people. If you want the tallest building in town, do you build a strong tall building or do you try to knock down everybody else's buildings? Recession or not, prestige cars continue to appeal to the very rich. A new £1.2 million Aston Martin, the One-77, attracted 100 buyers for the 77 cars (hence its name) that were to be manufactured. No such waiting list though for the Renault 1.8 Million.

However, despite all this focus upon cars, there are alternative transport options, although you wouldn't think this on the roads at 8.30 a.m. on a Monday morning. I'm sure you have noticed that when the children are on holiday suddenly there is absolutely no rush-hour traffic at all. The difference in volume between normal school-run days and school holidays is stark in the extreme. It's not helped by ladies taking their children to school in those huge 4 × 4s which are better suited to a four-week expedition across the Sahara rather than a four-mile round trip to St Mary's Primary School.

It can be dangerous on the roads and the Department of Transport's National Travel Survey in 2007 found that 7 per cent of all adults surveyed had suffered a road accident in the proceeding 12 months. However, one quite amazing statistic is that the number of pedestrian fatalities has fallen by 78 per cent over the last 40 years. The number of road casualties in 2007 was 248,000 and the number of fatalities 2,946, which encouragingly means that only just over

1 in a 100 people involved in a road accident pass away. For the families of the 2,946, who no doubt never truly recover from the tragedy and trauma, it is 2,946 too many.

Having driven in the US and Britain I was very surprised to find the US fatality rate of 14.3 per 100,000 of population is nearly three times our rate of 5.4 per 100,000. In the US, especially away from big cities, driving is so much more relaxed than in the UK. No one races away from traffic lights and people just seem to meander around. When you jump in your car at Heathrow Airport long-term car park you can almost feel the Goofy rise in you! However, the facts seem to speak for themselves, although I suspect our statistics are underpinned more by the fact that most of the time there isn't enough room on Britain's roads to get up enough speed before the next roundabout or traffic jam.

Do you remember comedian Jasper Carrot used to feature real-life motor insurance claims in his act? Here are a few new examples: 'I pulled into the lay-by with smoke coming from under the bonnet. I realised the car was on fire so I took my dog and smothered it with a blanket'; 'In an attempt to kill a fly, I drove into a telegraph pole'; and, finally, 'No one was to blame for the accident but it would never have happened if the other driver had been alert.'

To get to a stage where you can have an accident and submit a claim, you have to pass the dreaded driving test. The Driving Standards Agency report that in the financial year 2007/08 there were 1,829,000 driving tests completed in the UK and I assume by their emphasis on 'completed' they specifically exclude those where the learner driver crashed or abandoned the vehicle in frustration! The average pass rate is 44 per cent with the theory test pass rate approximately 75 per cent. It's worth questioning how genuinely valuable the driving test is, as it seems to include so many things you never repeat in your real-life driving career; three-point turns, emergency stops when someone hits the dashboard and, dare we admit it, indicating and looking in your mirrors.

The most hated of all motoring-related people must be traffic wardens. In Torquay, Devon traders became so incensed by the negative effect that parking tickets were having on trade that many of them banned traffic wardens from their premises and this included a charity shop! The *Daily Telegraph* reported one case where traffic wardens were stoned by parents at a number of primary schools in one road in Brentwood Essex, in an incident that was like a throwback to biblical times. One parent was quoted as saying, 'I come here an hour early to get a spot – it's crazy.' Whatever happened to school buses?

It just can't be fun being a traffic warden unless of course you love the power, the uniform and the judgemental nature of your job. Their uniform just doesn't help, as it encourages motorists' resistance to perceived authoritarian unreasonableness. In fact, a Tory-led council in West Sussex rebranded its wardens as 'parking advisers'. This is interesting and I do see where they are coming from with this reframing, but 'advisers' – surely not?

Technology has changed so many of our motoring experiences and the best of these improvements is that cars today are generally very reliable. This was not always the case and in times gone by motoring was more of a variable activity. Today we have an automatic choke, power steering and air bags, all to help make driving more reliable and secure, and of course that most exciting of inventions, satellite navigation.

Don't you just love these gadgets? My satnav is a woman and I have to say is suitably unpredictable and temperamental. Some days she is all chatty and friendly and gets me where I want to go with a cheery voice and no complications whatsoever. Other days, oh dear! On these days she will go all retro on me and forget every one of the modern road systems, so I will be happily driving along the A34 and suddenly she decides to forget the dual carriageway ever existed and I get the dreaded 'You have left the recognised road system'. Help! Not only are we lost, but we have left planet Earth!

On her bad days she will refuse to accept that I know a better and faster way, so no matter how far I drive down my route, she keeps telling me to go back to her way-off-line route, and on her *really* bad days insists, and I'm sure her voice changes tonality to a short-sharp grumpy tone, 'Please make a U-turn, immediately', but she sometimes leaves out the 'please' and emphasises 'immediately'.

My satellite navigation system has a name, in deference to a dream my wife once had. One morning she woke up (my wife that is, not my satnav) and I noticed that she seemed unusually annoyed with me and therefore I asked her why. She said she was annoyed with me because she had had a dream that night in which I had been unfaithful with a woman (whom I have never met) named Helen. Does this ever happen to you – you innocently sleep through the night and then get blamed for your spouse's disconcerting dream? My wife has always said I treat my satellite navigation system like a real person and so to teach them both a lesson I called my satnav Helen.

Satellite navigation can get you to where you want to go but it can't protect you from our more appalling driving behaviours. These are some of the most annoying of fellow motorist's behaviours which I'm sure you recognise: driving towards you on full beam ('I can't see a bleeping thing'); motorway middle lane cruising ('I'll show him, I will overtake and cut back in front of him'); spraying their windscreen washers on a dry day to clean the dead flies from their windscreens and putting water all over your car ('Is that rain?'); not turning off their indicators so that they are continually turning right for five miles ('Flash them – to let them know'); hooting their horn because you waited two seconds before pulling away at green traffic lights ('Patience – I was only daydreaming about marquetry'); not saying 'thank you' when you let them out from a road junction ('How ignorant – some people!'); and the most unpleasant of all, picking their nose as they drive towards you, in the certain knowledge no one can see them ('Yes, we can!').

With the recession in full swing, record numbers of us took our 2010 summer holidays back home in Britain. This brings back worrying memories of summer holidays past and leaving home at 4 a.m. to avoid the inevitable three-hour traffic jam on the Honiton bypass, which brings us suitably to the next subject: holidays.

14

We're Going on Holiday

My formative years came just before the age of overseas packaged holidays and as a result going on holiday back then inevitably involved car journeys, although like most of us I have since earnestly made up for all this lost time.

In fact no other area of our lives better illustrates how modern society has changed than that of travel. During my early childhood years overseas travel was never a possibility for any of my family. My dad had travelled extensively with the Services and of course, like most post-war wives, my mum had never left the country and I'm sure this was very typical of their whole generation. I didn't travel overseas myself until I was aged 22 and then only to Paris. However, thanks to people like Thomas Cook, Fred Laker and Cosmos, everything changed and at quite a pace, although sadly Freddie wasn't able to see the result of his groundbreaking business.

For my generation and particularly those belonging to the classic middle-income families, overseas holidays became standard practice. Indeed my parents' generation suddenly became the world's most seasoned leisure travellers. Once they retired they had time and disposable income, and my goodness were they in the mood to catch up for all those lost working-class years. My parents vacationed to Florida, Malta, Spain, Bulgaria, Cyprus, to the former Yugoslavia and even took a month away every winter in the warmth of the Canary Islands. They weren't on their own either and in fact it felt like a whole generation just made up for lost time and took to the air.

For my children's generation this new era meant that from an early age they saw much of the world, or more accurately, they saw a lot of hotel kids' clubs and pretty young Scandinavian nannies. Once they became independent their generation then took travel to a new level. With a refined taste for travel developed from an early age, a fortnight's packaged holiday in Minorca was not for this bunch. It was off on camel treks through the Sahara, staying in YMCAs in Thailand, Sydney and Singapore, although like a salmon returning to its mother and father's spawning grounds, they almost instinctively ended up returning to Cornwall, by flocking to the ultimate wild destination of Newquay!

However, what goes around often comes around, and we seem to be entering a new era that, owing to economic conditions, once again involves the prospect of British seaside holidays. For those of my generation this would involve a return to forgotten experiences involving memories of endless traffic jams through narrow A roads, buckets and spades, toffee apples, candyfloss, deckchairs, Punch and Judy shows, beach pebbles from small to large, end-of-pier variety shows, caravans, fish n' chips, sandy picnics, beach balls, cockles and whelks, windbreaks, Mr Softy 99 cones, amusement arcades and – how this works I don't know – but memories of whole days of torrential rain and acute sunburn on the same holiday. The memory is a funny thing, isn't it?

If we are coming back home to holiday then a whole new generation will discover what constitutes the great British traditional seaside holiday and all its idiosyncrasies. Isn't the 'bucket and spade' an odd phenomenon? Whoever first thought that taking an array of mock DIY tools on holiday was a great leisure idea? As a child, I vividly remember sitting for hours on the beach excavating huge trenches, digging drainage ditches, constructing levees and building those strange featureless turrets. We all did this and, from one end of the beach to the other, children and their dads were busy practising grand engineering projects, the like of which you would get EU funding for today.

The best construction projects had running water in the little moats around the castle walls and included bridges made of ice lolly sticks that linked each of the faceless turrets. We would spend hours building our own little sandy Camelot, until the inevitable result – the tide came in and washed it all away leaving behind only a small rounded wet mound of sand. Why didn't my dad have sufficient engineering foresight to realise that all we needed to do was set up our construction project above the tideline?

What about candyfloss and toffee apples? How on earth will they survive our health-addicted modern society? Both treats are basically lumps of sugar, one welded on to a piece of fruit on a stick and the other coloured pink and blown up to appear significantly more substantial than it really is. I hesitate to think how many calories there are in a toffee apple but I'm fairly sure your dentist wouldn't approve. Will these two bastions of the seaside holiday survive our health microscope? Or, as with almost everything else nowadays, will they need re-engineering? In today's health-crazed world we will probably evolve to a higher plane and create new light treats, involving saccharine-covered apples on a stick and soya floss, but they don't sound in the least bit appetising, do they?

I'm surprised that deckchairs didn't become extinct years ago. Is there a more uncomfortable seating device available on this earth than a deckchair? First of all they test your DIY skills to the limit just erecting them in the correct position and then to sit in one you have to take a leap of faith, like a free-fall parachutist, and plonk your bottom into the awaiting hollow of canvas. Once settled in, you can't actually move as you are fixed rigidly between the two wooden constraints either side of you. However, getting out of a deckchair is the greatest challenge of all, as you need to lift yourself from approximately two inches above ground to full standing height. Its great exercise for those arm muscles though and a chance to work off those candyfloss calories. On behalf of these relics of Victoriana it has to be said that deckchairs stack great, are waterproof and are cheap to make, although I suggest you enjoy them this time around, as it could be your last chance.

If ever anything is a leftover from our ancient Victorian seaside culture, it's Punch and Judy shows. These violent portrayals of spousal abuse are definitely not politically correct and no doubt, once it realises what actually happens in them, the EU will ban them for good. I have an idea how we might revitalise these ancient seaside children's entertainments by bringing them up-to-date and making them more relevant to today's children. We need to throw away all those Victorian gowns and hats and replace them with tracksuits and baseball caps. We also need to replace that outdated rolling pin with an up-to-date baseball bat. If we throw in some drugs, alcohol and teen parents we would have our very own new seaside 'Jerry and Kyle' show and this could work!

One place where you wouldn't be surprised to encounter juvenile problem children is in a seaside amusement arcade, which can feel a little dark and menacing and perhaps less than amusing. As a child my mum warned me of unsavoury men who might approach me from within these potential dens of iniquity and whisk me away from her. More than likely my own memories are also tarnished by the huge monetary cost of amusing my children by letting them roam, accompanied of course, in amusement arcades on rainy days in Bournemouth. Most children now have all the games at home on their laptop, or more than likely with them on their mobile phone, so surely these amusement arcades are coming under increasing commercial threat, which is no doubt to my mum's great relief.

I'm sure there are people out there who are connoisseurs of cockles, although in my experience these unattractive shellfish normally include a good dose of gritty sand. Isn't consuming a whelk like chewing on vinegar-tasting bite-sized pieces of inner tube? Fish n' chips are of course a different matter altogether – can there be a better out-of-doors eating experience than this? The greasier, the better, and isn't that the point? It's the decadence that appeals.

Quite frankly they could put anything inside the batter, as you can't taste anything when you bite into the white flesh. It tastes of, well, nothing; but put it between some greasy batter and you have one of the world's great outdoors dining experiences. This is why cod and plaice cooked on their own always need sauces. If we agreed to waive all niceties of trade description in order that we could put any fish we wanted in between the batter, we could solve all the world's over-fishing issues in one fishy swoop of the net. As long as it comes out of the water that's all that matters, it's fish. I'm certain that if we were fed alternative delicacies, all wrapped up in some delicious greasy, salty batter, accompanied by a suitably soggy bag of chips and washed down by a nice can of Diet Coke (you have to watch your weight, don't you?), we would love it just as much and we would save the planet at the same time.

The following are included in a list of fish available for us to feast upon. These have been given a rating of 1 or 2 by the Marine Conservation Society, which believes, that they 'are fished within sustainable levels using methods which do not cause unacceptable damage to the environment'. We could try these exciting alternatives: pollock and chips, gurnard and chips, or even whiting and chips. We could even use freshwater fish and feast on carp and chips. All these dishes are fish and chips, so let's stop being fussy and go green – us that is, not the fish!

It was the Victorians who invented seaside holidays and particularly bathing in the sea. This was an interesting concept because the English Channel, even at the height of summer, is quite frankly cold and far removed from the warmth of the clear blue Mediterranean. However, it's all we have got and the Victorians didn't have St-Tropez so they made do with Brighton, and why not? But don't stay in too long.

When my family visited the beach my mum was always protecting our well-being by reminding us that you must never swim until a full hour had elapsed after eating. A lot of mums seem to have the same passionate belief in this holiday health truism. We all dutifully obeyed, as rebellion was never on the cards (it was too dangerous), but I have found nothing in my research to confirm the reliability of this old wives' tale. More relevant to our modern binge-drinking world is the advice, 'Don't swim when drunk', because the Isle of Wight might look close from Lymington beach after you have downed half a dozen tequila shots but it's actually over five miles away!

A more practical danger when on a British beach is getting into trouble in the sea swimming after a beach ball that is floating out on its way to France, Norway or Ireland. The ball never seems to get close enough to grab but always draws you further out to sea. At some stage you have to decide whether it's safer to swim back and leave the ball to its own fate or just jump on to the ball and await your inevitable fate as a star guest on one of those reality TV search-and-rescue programmes.

Today British beaches are much cleaner and more hygienic than they were in my childhood days where, when bathing, little brown soldiers were a constant threat. Nowadays I don't know where all the soldiers and bombers have gone but quite frankly I don't care, as long as it's not in my direction. Today all you need to worry about on our beaches are condoms and used heroin needles, which are still someone else's unpleasant and dangerous bodily fluids.

Whether we are flocking back home for our holidays or not, the evidence is that travel abroad is still big business. According to Directgov, in 2006 nearly 70 million trips were made overseas by British residents, of which approximately four out of five were for leisure. Possibly the continuing effects of sexism in the workplace, or perhaps mothers deciding not to travel away from their children, has meant that of the 8.9 million business trips abroad, only one in five was endured by women. In fact the National Travel Survey 2007 found that nearly half of all respondents had made an international flight from Great Britain within the last 12 months. Compare this to the USA where apparently only 34 per cent of people have passports, let alone actually travel out of the country, although to be fair they have more choice in the US for homeland vacations: the Colorado Rockies, New York, San Francisco, Florida's beaches, Alaska's wilderness, Yellowstone Park and California's Pacific coast, to name just a few.

Despite our American cousins' extensive choices at home, 3.6 million of them did decide to visit us and give us some of their dollars, making them our biggest tourist fans. The UK had 32.8 million visitors in 2007, which is approximately half of our population, so it's little wonder it gets crowded on our little island.

145

When one reviews the historical hard facts regarding holidays taken by us British, the economic and sociological changes really do become obvious. In 1987 British citizens' overseas travel hit its peak, but even in 1987 more people were holidaying at home than did in 1960. In fact incredibly six times more people holidayed at home in Britain in 1987 than did in 1960. Today we truly do have significantly greater leisure time.

However, when one compares the commercial reality of annual spending on holidays at home in Britain by its own citizens then the truth dawns. In 1997 we spent almost exactly the same at home on holidays as in the year 1951 and that's pound for pound. Unfortunately, a pound in 2007 is worth considerably less in buying power than it was in 1951. We are going abroad in our droves for our main holiday and spending some money on the side at home on short breaks. It's akin to a cad of a husband taking his wife out for a meal, to keep the interest alive, but taking her to a burger bar and then splashing out on a four-star luxury restaurant for the secretary – poor form indeed. Does this mean that, owing to the credit crunch, it will be the end of slap-up meals for 'that woman' and back to romantic dining at home?

A holiday *Which?* report in 2006 voted Whitby as Britain's top resort and, given that Whitby is located on Britain's windy east coast and adjoining the North Sea, this is a major achievement. Whitby has an incredible 550,000 visitors a year and a population of only 14,500, which must make it one of the worst places in the world to ask directions – the chances are the person you ask won't live there. One-fifth of the local residents work directly in the tourist industry and no doubt virtually all the other industries in Whitby service the tourist industry. What an achievement! It's a great British success. I say make the local council's head of tourism the Chancellor of the Exchequer, though we'll have to remember to keep an eye out for their expenses on that second home in Sea View Drive.

Whitby might have its supporters but there is no doubt whatsoever which resort is Britain's number-one most visited town and that is the mighty Blackpool. This resort, despite its location on England's rainy north-west coast – and let's face it if you were an entrepreneur planning to set up Britain's top resort with a clean piece of paper, this location would not be your first choice – is an unmitigated commercial success. Blackpool's statistics defy logic and yet every year they consistently deliver tourist success: nearly 100,000 holiday beds, 1 million ice creams eaten and over 1 million sticks of rock crunched. Blackpool's statistics really are incredible.

Since 1934 the resort's famed illuminations have been officially opened and 'switched on' by many famous men, women, puppets and horses. It may seem strange to talk of being switched on by a puppet, and it's an even stranger thought that Red Rum once switched on the lights; I assume with a dextrous hoof! The list of dignitaries endowed with this honour reflect their times: George Formby (1953), Sir Matt Busby (1968 – Manchester United's first European Cup-winning year), Rear Admiral Sandy Woodward (1982 – he was the Falklands Task Force Commander-in-Chief) and amazingly in 1955, right in the middle of the Cold War, Jacob Malik, the then Russian ambassador. Blackpool really did its bit trying to improve world peace.

Most telling of all as to how our world has changed is the list of people who officially opened the illuminations in the last 15 years, because in every single year the chosen people have been pop stars, with the exception of that time-traveller, Doctor Who. Celebrity rules in Britain's prime resort, like everywhere else. If Blackpool ever gets the concession for a super-casino it will be on course to become our very own 'Lanc Vegas', Elton John, Céline Dion, Cirque du Soleil and all.

Tourism is big money for a country's economy and in 2007 the World Tourism Organisation reported that France was the most visited country with 81.9 million tourist arrivals. Although we only had 30.7 million visitors we did rank sixth in the world and, importantly, ahead of Australia. However, who do you think gets their visitors to spend the most money during their visit? No surprises here – of course those magicians of marketing, the USA. On average in 2007 each international tourist visiting the USA spent 42 per cent more than each tourist visiting the UK. It seems we could do better and perhaps we might start with our customer service.

The country's citizens that spend the most on their holidays are the Germans with a huge $82.9 billion spent and you can now see why the Spanish hoteliers put up with the Germans and their 5.15 a.m. towel-laying rituals – money talks. However, don't despair; we came third as the biggest spenders at $72.3 billion dollars.

According to Forbes Traveller the fourth most visited attraction in the world is good old Trafalgar Square. I travel through Trafalgar Square regularly and not once have I ever thought of it as ahead of these exotic destinations as an international tourist visitor's Mecca: Disneyland California, the Great Wall of China, the Louvre, the Eiffel Tower, the Grand Canyon, Vatican City, Niagara Falls, Sydney Opera House, the Colosseum and Notre-Dame, but it is. For all the Eiffel Tower's pomp, fame and majesty, over twice as many foreign visitors are drawn to Trafalgar Square. When it comes to attracting international visitors, Nelson's Column, the now unfed pigeons and the National Gallery do it, Rule Britannia!

We spend a huge amount of money on holidays and travel, but why do we do it? Is it to add to our education and broaden our mind? Is it to enjoy different climates, cultures and food, or is it just to get away from it all? My own experiences of holidays are that much of the enjoyment is derived from the planning and anticipation of the trip. Am I alone in finding that the actual experience sometimes involves a significant degree of stress, anxiety and disappointment? Air travel has a big part to play in much of this anxiety and yet we keep on going back for more. When you arrive at the airport you can feel your stress levels rising. 'Where is check-in area H?' 'Do we have seats together?' 'Is my baggage under the excess weight limit?' 'Am I in the shortest queue?' 'Am I in the correct queue?' It's all very worrying!

Have you noticed how the check-in desk people take your

documents and then engage in a whirlwind of keyboard tapping that can't possibly be all to do with your booking? It's as if they are typing up a few pages of *War and Peace*, not entering a few key digits from your booking form. Perhaps they take time out while you are waiting to visit their Facebook page, or have the airlines created a complex system that makes us all think it is far more complicated than it really is? You can't interrupt them though. Ask a question while they are in full tap and you are bound to get one of those looks.

I love the inane questions you get asked that can't possibly ever get a 'Yes'. The best question of all is: 'Has anyone tampered with your bag?' Now you're not going to say in response, 'Goodness knows' or worse still, 'Yes, but who cares?' Better still is the US Department of Homeland Security's Form I-94W, Welcome to the United States, which cunningly asks, 'Have you ever been or are you now involved in espionage or sabotage, or in terrorist activities?' There is room for only a 'Yes' or a 'No' answer but no room for a 'Not sure'! This crafty question must fool a few terrorists.

It has to be acknowledged that you can understand why foreign airlines would want to delay the arrival of the hordes from Britain. However proud one is to be British, one has to admit that our compatriots abroad are not always a credit to their nation. Their desire to fill Spanish resorts with the worst of British cuisine like greasy eggs and chips and to display acres of reddened paunch to all who don't wish to see is not particularly attractive to our European neighbours. Our behaviour is not improved by our apparent prime goal, which is to export our well-practised binge-drinking culture. This seems to have taken over from the knotted handkerchief as the least attractive of British exports.

It's not that you don't find rows of greasy fast-food outlets in British high streets or that you don't see hordes of drunken youngsters on the street every night of the week. The problem is that when we travel abroad we become more aware of our position as representatives of our nation, of our *Britishness*. Thus, under this type of self-awareness, our embarrassment is inevitable.

Unfortunately, when we travel to the USA and experience what the best of their tourism offers (such as Disney's Magic Kingdom in Florida), we might feel even more ashamed of our nation's service levels. The comparison between the customer service you receive in America's most basic outlets and the service we offer all customers in the UK is stark. We all know that in the US when they say 'Have a nice day', they don't really mean it, but is this true? They don't get paid a high basic rate of pay and most of their earnings are from tips and therefore perhaps they do mean it – *your* good day means *their* good day! Whether they do mean it or not, it feels good to be treated well, and hence that feeling of embarrassment at our often appalling service at home.

People behave very differently when they are abroad on holiday and perhaps this is the attraction, being different, acting differently and importantly doing it somewhere else. I find that the first two days of my holiday are spent getting used to 'not being at work'. After three days I am really getting into the relaxed holiday way and by week two I'm really engaged with the whole process of strolling, eating, drinking and lying around reading. You see, if you persevere with something long enough, you will eventually succeed.

Have you also noticed how, when you have been away on holiday, on your return it feels like you have been away for a month or more? This is even if you have just been away for a few days. However, when your friends and family have been away on their holiday and on their return they ask you, 'So what's happened while we've been away?', you say, 'Well, nothing really', because it feels like they have only been gone a couple of days. Time is a complex phenomenon.

There are a few days a year that are enjoyed as holidays by almost everyone and these are those particularly British phenomena, the Bank Holidays. Many people don't really appreciate the intricacies of cricket but this may well change when they realise that we have cricket to thank for our Bank Holidays – no, honestly! The first legislation relating to Bank Holidays was passed by Sir John

Lubbock in 1871 and Sir John was an enthusiast of cricket and felt Bank of England employees should have the opportunity to participate in and attend cricket when the matches were scheduled. English people were caught out by this generosity, so bowled over and stumped for a name that they originally called Bank Holidays St Lubbock's Days.

Until 1971 we didn't even have New Year's Day or May Day as Bank Holidays, but some foresighted politician anticipated the country's binge-drinking future and decided we should add these two days to recover from our hangovers. We take Bank Holidays very seriously in the UK and when a Bank Holiday falls on a weekend we get a Royal Proclamation to move it to a weekday. This beats our European neighbours who completely lose their public holidays when they fall on a weekend and I say a hearty 'God bless the Queen!'

As the recession has seemingly moved travellers back to more traditional retro UK holiday experiences, I expect other former glories may be restored including that of the bed and breakfast. The Internet has already done wonders for B&Bs because the biggest problem with them is the fear of the unknown and at least with such wholesale Internet access you can now find choices, in the location you want, view some pictures and importantly read of others' experiences. As a result the old caricature of the dragon landlady in curlers is surely long since passed, isn't it?

Previously, like many of us, I wouldn't have dreamed of staying at a B&B, but the Internet's lure did its trick and I found myself enjoying one such example of today's modern guest house experience. It was an attractive house in the country, in need of some TLC perhaps, but clean, competitively priced, and with mainly positive reviews from previous visitors. I should have realised there wasn't a hotel experience on the way when in the establishment's email response to my booking I was told I had to check in between 5 and 7 p.m., no earlier and no later.

When I arrived at 5.30 p.m. I couldn't rouse the hostess, despite banging on doors and roving the house. I eventually got her attention and, once I was let in, the room was very pleasant, although memories came flooding back of B&Bs past when I saw a number of printed signs in the bedroom and bathroom. One said: 'Do not put anything down the toilet other than toilet paper.' This is all very well but what about my aching bowels? Another was in Japanese as well as English and asked Japanese visitors to 'Please bathe in the European style not the Japanese style.' This really got my imagination running. What was it about the Japanese style of bathing that would create chaos in sleepy Devon? Yet another note instructed you not to 'pull hard on the rope in the bathroom as the light is activated by the light switch outside the bathroom'. The place was an endless list of rules and regulations culminating with my discovery that you couldn't pay by credit card; it had to be cash. I fear that we can start to expect more of this if we really go retro with B&Bs.

Staying in a guesthouse really is like staying over at a friend's or acquaintance's house, which is perfectly acceptable if you know them or like them. Unfortunately, with guesthouses you take pot luck. Typically, all over the house are personal pictures and mementoes and it feels quite frankly a little embarrassing. Don't you feel like you are intruding into someone's life and you find yourself speaking in hushed tones as a sign of respect? It's a strange experience and I hesitate to imagine what our overseas Japanese visitors make of such odd places to rest their heads. Perhaps we should leave them some signs on the wall to instruct them on B&B decorum.

When you stay in local B&Bs or quaint country hotels, isn't the biggest disappointment of all often the much anticipated Full English Breakfast? You have visions of the host waking early to go down to the chicken shed to pick up the newly laid eggs from those frolicking free-range hens, all with their own names, buying locally produced sausages from the village's jolly butcher, baking their own bread from scratch and so on. Unfortunately, the reality is usually somewhat different and often includes button mushrooms, super-market 'value' bacon, thinly sliced economy bread and fishy-tasting eggs, all microwaved to boiling point. I particularly dislike the hard crust a reheated microwaved sausage develops. Perhaps I'm just plain unlucky.

However, they very nearly get away with this poor-quality food by the exaggerated descriptions that always adorn them; 'Hearty Scottish Breakfast', 'Locally Produced West Country Breakfast', 'Traditional Irish Breakfast' and, of course, 'Home-cooked Cots-wolds Produce'. Who could resist these titles?

So much for retro holidays but what does the future have in store for us in terms of tomorrow's holidays? Space tourism already exists, albeit at a cost that isn't yet affordable for 99.9 per cent of the population. Underwater hotels are already being built and at the time of writing one such hotel, Hydrolis, is due to open 66 feet below the surface of the Persian Gulf in Dubai in 2010, a rival to the underwater Lost Chamber Suites in the £750-million New Atlantis Hotel that already exists in the same resort. Will we go back to eco-friendly airships or will we replace actual travel with virtual online experiences? Whatever the future holds there is plenty of money to be made from our desire to get away from it all, which brings us suitably to the next subject: business.

15

It's a Deal Then

One of the industries that has been most affected by technology is that of travel agencies, with the Internet dramatically changing our holiday buying patterns. The all-day Saturday visit to the travel agent, sitting at a desk poring over brochures, to book your two-week package holiday in Greece has long since gone, and personally I miss that excitement.

Today you are much more likely to surf the Web to get the best deals on flights, prebook your ferry from the mainland to your island of choice and handpick your room in the hotel having scrolled through the handy virtual tour and read a number of real-life customer reviews. How times have changed, as has the way we do business.

Making money is obviously the main objective of being in business, but whenever money is involved it always gets complicated. Most of us understand why business owners would want to be rich, and wouldn't we all? However, the path to this goal can be varied and not without the need for some luck and a number of sacrifices, preferably lifestyle, not sheep! I have spent many of my working years advising and helping businesses and in my experience there are a number of ways to achieve the goal of great personal wealth but let's have some fun though and simplify it a little.

One way to get rich is to be what we might call a Miser-Dictator (MD). Miser-Dictators are the people most likely to gain great wealth, as their chosen path involves a lifetime of extraction; taking from customers, taking from suppliers, taking from staff, taking from partners, basically taking from everyone. Theirs is a life of miserly loneliness driven by a dogged belief that you must never show weakness and that they are always right, as once on this path there is no room for self-doubt. History is full of examples of such people; you might have met one or two yourself and, let's be honest, they are often very unpleasant macho men or sometimes women trying very hard to be the worst of men.

Before you decide to be a Miser-Dictator and join the stampede for great riches, it's worth considering the downside of this path. I have always found this type of person to be exceptionally unhappy, unfulfilled and always lonely. They have no one with which to share their wealth, because most people don't stay around long enough, and they simply don't know how to enjoy anything in life, let alone the opportunities great wealth brings. Being a Miser-Dictator provides you with an excellent chance of wealth, but an almost certain loss of other kinds of richness in life. It's worth thinking about giving this one a miss as it probably doesn't justify the cost.

Another way to gain great wealth is to be what might be called a Passionate Aspirer (PA). Passionate Aspirers are people who have a burning desire to succeed and a form of evangelical belief in their ultimate success. These people are typically business owners and often engaging people, albeit, at their own admittance, somewhat compulsive and controlling. To succeed as a Passionate Aspirer you need to feel in control because then you can avoid those deadly self-doubts and insecurity, which for a Passionate Aspirer is like foot-and-mouth disease to a dairy farmer. Passionate Aspirers can also be called entrepreneurs and very often are leaders in our society, and frequently their success is underpinned by a large and well-developed ego. I like Passionate Aspirers because they are fun to be around; things are always happening and they don't blame anyone but themselves. In fact, they make things happen.

A further way to have great wealth is by becoming a Happy Random (HR). Happy Randoms are people who by sheer luck find themselves in receipt of sudden riches. Typically this is by winning the lottery, the death of a rich relative, winning the football pools or a similar stroke of financial good fortune. Other more obscure methods include finding the county council suddenly making the field you own at the bottom of your garden Designated Development Land, or finding an antique watch in your garage in Peckham that's worth millions of pounds and auctioning it at Sotheby's. Another way to become a Happy Random is to meet the man or woman of your dreams and find they are very rich; by chance of course.

A few years ago according to a Camelot-commissioned survey, a total of 1,800 millionaires had been created by the National Lottery since its inception. This is only approximately 1 in every 300 of our UK millionaires, so don't hold your breath for this route to riches as the odds are definitely against you! Normally becoming rich by being a Happy Random involves pure chance and no real input from you, unless of course, you are a gold-digger and, if you are, then God rest your soul.

Another alternative route to riches is being a Family Downer (FD). Family Downers are people who by genetic fate are the offspring of any one of Miser-Dictators, Passionate Aspirers or Happy Randoms. Thus, simply by the receipt of their parents' wealth they themselves become wealthy and this offers endless opportunities for games of dominoes in luxury hotels with bowling alleys in their rooms. Typically, Family Downers readily indulge themselves in their wealth and the trappings of great riches, having been brought up to live the high life and all this entails, and they frequently have no comprehension of what their parents went through before them; in the case of MDs – misery and coercion; PAs – sacrifice and commitment; HRs – luck and more luck!

Some Family Downers do carry on the good work – 'My dad always said you can't trust anyone' (MDs); 'My parents always taught me to provide for myself and believe in my own success' (PAs); 'My mum always told me that when you get lucky, don't fight it, enjoy it' (HRs) – but most don't and like the rest of us they muddle along through life making of it what they can, just with more money.

Like Del Boy in *Only Fools and Horses*, many of us have a wish to be rich: 'One day we are going to be millionaires.' The reality is that the vast majority of wealthy people achieve their wealth by being a Passionate Aspirer and building a successful business over many years. Coutts & Co. is often seen as the bank of the rich and the Royals and in 2004 their survey showed that an amazing 50 per cent or more of people believed they may become a millionaire in their lifetime. Coutts estimated that the money needed to live the millionaire lifestyle of luxury home, cars, apartment abroad and extensive holidays, was today more akin to a net wealth of £2.6 million rather than the traditional £1 million. Another surprising fact contained in this survey was that the average millionaire family still had a 50-per-cent mortgage on their main home. So much for that much-quoted ultimate goal to be mortgage-free!

However, the credit crunch, falling property prices and stock market values has reduced the number of millionaires in Britain and, according to the Centre for Economics and Business Research; this has fallen from its peak in 2004 of 489,000 to a 2007 figure of 242,000 millionaires.

If you do make it and become a millionaire, then the next problem is how to comfortably mix with your peers and such varied bedfellows as MDs, PAs, HRs and FDs. The first problem is that MDs don't like anyone at all; PAs often pretend to love you but when it comes to the crunch, it's not true; HRs do not understand the real world anymore and FDs are always so miserable, especially considering they're so privileged.

Irrespective of the number of millionaires in the country, without a shadow of a doubt, the best and most likely way to achieve this status is as a Passionate Aspirer and thus our interest in all things business. TV programmes like *The Apprentice* and *Dragons' Den* catch people's imagination by offering us the chance to be voyeurs of some of the more whacky potential Passionate Aspirers who in turn are judged by some proven Passionate Achievers.

Most of us in this country have some interaction or interest in the workings of businesses. We either own a business, work for an owner-managed business, work for a large organisation, or, if we work in the public sector, have regular contact with businesses by purchasing goods and services from them. In our Western capitalist and highly commercial society you simply can't escape business, and it won't let you!

The reality is that the business community employs four out of five of all people who work in the UK. Small businesses that have fewer than ten people employ nearly half of all private-sector employees. In the UK, according to the National Statistics Office, in June 2009 we had approximately 2.1 million businesses registered for VAT or PAYE and NIC. A total of 57 per cent were corporations, 14 per cent partnerships and 25 per cent of people went it alone as sole proprietors. An amazing 98 per cent of all registered businesses employed fewer than 50 employees and, of those, 89 per cent employed fewer than ten employees. Interestingly only 9 per cent of all businesses are retail operations, which means we have a business support function to back up the retailers at a ratio of nine to one. It's all a magically complex structure to keep the capitalist engine going. The whole infrastructure is so beautifully and finely balanced it's no wonder we occasionally have a few hiccups like the credit crunch.

Being employed by each of these sizes of enterprises offers a wide range of different and fascinating working experiences. If you see your working life as a journey then what ship you choose for your sea cruise is very relevant. Working in the public sector involves the traditional job security and bureaucracy. Public-sector entities are similar to oil tankers – almost impossible to sink even in the roughest seas. They're slow and cumbersome, there's room for plenty of wasted storage space on board, and you are never really sure who is in charge, but a great and safe way to travel the high seas, except of course that you need to stay well clear of other oil tankers!

Large corporate businesses are similar to sleek and glossy cruise liners, all fancy receptions, mountains of shining glass, and safe in a storm but only if they put the stabilisers out and the captain is good at his job. They're more fun on the top deck than the bottom, a little impersonal, but once you know how to get about, you can see a lot and learn how to sit around not doing much!

Small businesses are like motorboats that come in many different sizes. They're fast, adaptable and can change direction at any time.

It can get a bit rocky if the seas get rough and unfortunately some do sink. You get to know the crew really well and if you have a good skipper it can be a great journey, but watch out for the wake from those cruise liners as it can be vicious if they cut across your bow.

If you are tragically unemployed, the water can be a lonely and dangerous place in which to be stranded. In this situation any ship will do and some people even start to build their own new speed boat, starting small, but soon adding a two-stroke engine … and you never know … one day. Before the credit crunch many of us may have taken our place on a craft for granted, but not now.

Whether you work on an oil tanker (in the public sector), a cruise liner (for a large corporation) or a motor boat (in an owner-managed business), employment offers a myriad of wonderful opportunities to laugh at yourself and your shipmates' bizarre and amusing interactions. Some oil tanker workers have the wonderful skill and technique that enables them to always look busy while having very little to do, or so it seems! The aim of many oil tanker workers appears to be to get through the day as easily as possible and if you can get up on top deck for a smoke every hour, so much the better.

Most of us have huge respect for National Health professionals who do a grand job for us all. They work in difficult conditions with a passion and commitment that is admirable and – lest we forget – most of their customers are ill! There is just one thing though: how is it, when you are patiently waiting in a hospital for someone such as a doctor, a nurse or a receptionist to deal with you, the place seems crowded out with doctors, nurses and receptionists – nearly always on the other side of the desk? For some reason none of the great raft of people walking around, joking, moving bits of paper or looking at things on the wall is apparently ever the right sort of person for your need. It's puzzling but I'm sure there is a reason, although isn't it a strange experience to be in the middle of such an apparently productive and active workplace, but none of it seemingly there to help you?

The Health Service does deliver something nearly as important as efficient patient care and that is as being the last bastion of paper in the workplace! Everywhere you look in the business world they are banning paper and the paperless office is the 'big idea' for the future, because we must save the planet as well as sell lots of widgets. Not so in the National Health Service where it seems a prerequisite when moving around a hospital is to have at least one piece of paper attached to a clipboard. One thing is for sure: paper still lives in the NHS – for now.

Cruise liner workers are very different from oil tanker workers. They both work on big hulks of ships but there the similarity ends. Oil tanker workers get dirty but cruise liner workers wear nice clothes and have their own little picnic areas called desks.

For some people working in this big-ship environment, the simple aim in your working life is twofold. One, take as much credit as you can for every success that's going, even if your involvement is peripheral (after all it's what being part of a team is all about!) Two, ensure no dirty excretion sticks on you when it hits the fan. Your personal mission statement is: 'It's not my fault! As you know, I was always a little unsure this would work.' Achieve these two goals and one day you could become a purser, first lieutenant or even captain. Unfortunately, it has to be said that all these office politics do take up a lot of time and energy, though of course the best cruise liners minimise this and get on with their journey without too much distraction.

Motor boats come in so many different sizes and types, with captains that range from tyrants of the high seas to lovely fluffy James Stewart types, that each working experience on one of these vessels is directly affected by the ship and its captain. Get a good ship and life can be huge fun; exhilarating speed-boat rides, journeys to beautiful tropical beaches that only motor boats can get to, and a chance to work closely with captains of industry and enjoy great camaraderie with other salty sea dogs. However, pick the wrong ship or get press-ganged and life can be hell working in these close quarters, so pick your boat well!

The uniforms worn by crew on these various types of vessels also vary wildly. Get on an old oil tanker and many of the crew will wear the sort of clothes they would at home while lounging on their couch watching television. On many ships smart-casual is the dress code of the day, except for the senior staff, who dress with authority (i.e. suits). Cruise liners tend to each have their own dress codes which are dictated by the latest fad of the time; dress-down Fridays or sometimes dress-down Mondays, Tuesdays, Wednesdays, Thursdays and Fridays.

The key to office dress code is to know what it is in advance and match everyone else, as nobody wants to be seen to be odd. There is nothing worse than going along to a sales meeting all dressed up in your smartest suit only to find it's 'Dress-down Tuesday' and your hosts are sat in designer denim jeans and T-shirts – or worse still, the reverse.

Whatever you wear to work, the first prerequisite is that you do wear something! With this in mind, have you ever had an airline lose your luggage? If you have, you will know that it's an appalling experience. I once experienced the delight of an American airline, which of course shall be nameless, losing my luggage for a ten-day business trip to the USA (US Airways actually – revenge is sweet!). I usually fly comfortably and thus I was suitably attired on the aeroplane in jeans and sweatshirt. I suffered the ignominy of that dreadful experience of standing beside the baggage conveyor belt staring forlornly at every piece of luggage as it slowly and sadly passed me by, until eventually there was just me and a couple of straggler pieces of luggage left. I knew then that our worst fear when flying (of course, strictly speaking, it's not this but actually crashing) had happened to me and I had become a Cinderella passenger – they had lost my bags and I wasn't going to the bags party. At the lost baggage desk I was promised by the airline that my bags had been found (I was supposed to feel good about this) and they were on their way from Denver to San Francisco to meet up with me once again in the Golden Gate City.

Needless to say, they didn't arrive and each day for the next three days I was promised they would be reunited with me, but every day – disappointment! Because I expected my clothes to arrive at any minute I kept delaying a trip to a Pier 49 clothes store and as a result I ended up at the plush 36th-floor headquarters of a large professional firm, with a panoramic view overlooking San Francisco Bay, Alcatraz and all that, in my smelly, grubby jeans and sweatshirt. However understanding my hosts were it was an extremely embarrassing and bizarre experience. How our dress code affects our attitude to work!

The great thing about business is that if it can happen, it will happen and therefore you never know what will occur next. Over the 25 years of running businesses and employing people I have had to deal with sexual harassment (woman to woman), alcoholism, violence, steaming affairs, stealing and even someone changing gender between going on holiday and returning! Where else could you gain such an insight into life's array of human behaviours? Mind you at the time, faced with the responsibility of dealing with the fallout from all this, I wasn't laughing at all.

It takes all types of people to work in an organisation, although whatever size of business you work in, everyone will recognise the classic bushwhacker type of fellow employee. These people are 'takers' who never genuinely add anything to the team. Figuratively, they spend most of their time hiding behind their desks, not showing their face, just occasionally peering out to the left or right but always keeping their head down. When you pass their desk every so often they jump up, point at you and say, 'I knew you shouldn't have done that,' and then they jump back behind their desk again. Bushwhackers never take responsibility for anything and I hate them! Sorry for this outburst, but I do.

Business is of course primarily about making profits and to find out if you have made a profit, we need financial statements prepared. Therefore, by definition, we need accountants and my confession is I was once such a person, so please avoid all thoughts of that traditional clichéd caricature. There was an episode of the American TV programme *Dallas* many years ago where the mogul bad brother JR Ewing needs to inspect this huge international oil company's finances. He calls down to the accountant and says, 'Brian, bring me the company books.' Brian arrives with a big thick ledger, JR scrolls down the page, says 'OK I see we aren't doing so good,' hands the ledger back and the plot continues. If only it was that simple, we wouldn't need accountants – but it isn't, so John Cleese can continue to have fun at accountants' expense.

Just in case you are feeling sorry for accountants, don't, because there is always tax to keep them occupied and none of us like paying tax, least of all businesses. Benjamin Franklin famously said, 'But in this world nothing is certain but death and taxes.' I have done some serious research on tax and after much analysis and consideration my results show that people who complain about how much tax they pay are broadly speaking split into two groups: men and women!

In fact, business gives us a great excuse to moan and complain, doesn't it? Unfortunately in business the behaviour of, let's just say, not always being completely honest, is more common than we would like to admit. This is evidenced by what I call the 'Three Great Business Lies'. Number one is 'I have started on it; I should have it with you shortly.' Number two is 'I have always been a team player' and, of course; number three is 'The cheque is in the post.'

How I yearn for the old days in business when, called by a client chasing for a report I had forgotten to do, I could say in a calm and assured manner, 'Yes, I'm waiting for that to be typed. It should be with you soon,' and then put the phone down and rush to start writing the report. Nowadays the client would say, 'No problem! I don't need a copy in Word, just scan the handwritten copy and email it to me now.' Today there is no escape. However, all this is academic because of course we would never tell a white lie like this, would we?

Progress being what it is, today you cannot get away with number three as easily as you could in times past either, because in the modern world they can ask you to cancel the cheque and do an online bank transfer – immediately! The old days in business were easier on the stress levels and in my opinion it is computers that are to blame for this change. Unlike the promises made to us in the 1980s, technology has not released us all to hours of new leisure time. What it has meant is that everything we do in business has to be more efficient and done in less time than previously and communicated at the speed of light. So much for all that leisure time we were promised.

When I was a young trainee my bosses regularly took long liquid lunches and their entertaining of clients and business contacts was extensive and lavish. Nowadays most people grab a sandwich at their desk while working on their emails. I remember hearing of one of my bosses flipping a coin with the client on a 'double or quits' basis at the end of one particularly liquid lunch and in respect of a project I and two others had worked on for a month. It was very disappointing for us to feel our endeavours could be so under-valued as to be gambled away. My boss won, but that's not the point!

This could not happen today, which in my mind is progress. There are other examples of progress. Juniors were then treated like latter-day slaves and had to run all manner of errands. We were even called by our surnames, like characters in *Tom Brown's School-days*: 'Walters, get me the brown nominal ledger!' Those were the days.

All businesses have customers of one kind or another and customer service is a key success factor in most businesses. As a regular customer of a range of varied businesses one has to say customer service in the UK can be varied. Clothes stores are the worst where the young till staff appear to have that amazing ability to turn you into the invisible man or woman. All they need to do to gain these magical powers is for a young colleague to stand beside them and start talking about last Saturday's binge-drinking session, or the problems which they are having with their boyfriend and, Ali Kazam, you're suddenly invisible. Not only that, but you seemingly become dumb, too. It doesn't matter what you say, they don't look at you or speak to you until miraculously they jump into life and suddenly say, 'Thank you for shopping at New Shop.' The classic frustrated response is, of course, 'Did your company get a refund?' To which the shop assistant's quizzical response will be 'To what?' and your winning answer is 'The customer service course you attended.' I know this is sarcastic but it's irritating to be ignored, isn't it?

English restaurants, especially branded chains, can be very irritating with their apparent inflexibility and particularly when you want something just slightly different. 'Could I have the chicken, please, but *without* the garlic sauce,' and the instant and pre-prepared answer is, 'I'm sorry we can't do this, as all our meals are pre-prepared.' How about those large DIY chain stores where you need to find a specific product you want to purchase (that is, pay them money) and you just can't find it in the row upon row of 20-feet-high racks? You hunt everywhere for a person in a grey T-shirt with that little logo on and when you do eventual find them hiding in the paint row, their enlightening answer is: 'If it's not on the shelf, we haven't got it.' Brilliant and how helpful. Whatever happened to those charming little local DIY stores where you could buy five screws without buying a packet of fifty, where they advised you on DIY and, best of all, that smell? There are still a few around and it's a joy when you find one. No doubt many are only kept running by increasing their overdraft, secured on the freehold property to finance their wages. What a shame, as you could while away a whole hour in an old-style hardware store.

In terms of customer service the ability to talk sensibly to customers is vital, which brings us suitably to the next subject: communication.

16

Listen and You Will Hear

They say the art of communication is listening and that is why we have two ears and one mouth, but using this genetic pre-planning assumption men would have three mouths (to get even more food and drink in) and only one ear.

In our technologically influenced modern world we now have an array of alternative methods of communication; blogs, Twitters, email, iPod downloads, mobile phones, texts, blackberries, Facebook, MSN Messenger, Skype and the quaint, but luckily not yet quite defunct, media known as letters and, of course, talking.

It's futile to fight progress and we all need to adapt to these ever-changing communication options. However, progress that involves a teenager sitting at a dinner table, ignoring her family and avoiding all conversation while continuously texting her school friends such gems of the English language as 'CU L8R' (see you later), has a questionable status as real progress. In fact 'texting' is highlighted on Microsoft's spell-check as a spelling error and they helpfully suggest a replacement spelling of 'taxing'. How appropriate!

It's hard to imagine but 20 years ago texting simply didn't exist – what is it about texts that so engages us and encourages such compulsive behaviour? You simply cannot leave a text unanswered, can you? When your mobile phone makes that familiar humming noise, suddenly you get a burning urge to look at your phone. You try to leave it alone, but that drive to look at the screen is huge. It's as if someone has sent you a message in a bottle and you are just leaving the bottle rolling around on the beach unanswered. You have just got to wade in, pick it up and look.

I assume this burning desire to look at our text messages comes from a primeval need to be loved and needed. If someone sends you a text, you must be loved; that is until you see it's from Voda-phone who are texting you to tell you, 'Congratulations, you have the right tariff.' Vodaphone loves me, hurrah!

Bill Gates needs to get Up 2 D8 with his spell-check and take out 'texting' as an error or he will be in business just to LOL (laugh out loud – is there any other way to laugh than out loud) or worse still ROFL (roll on the floor laughing – difficult to text at the same time though). TBH (to be honest – rather than lying) this is the problem with communication: it changes all the time and to survive you have to keep Up 2 D8. Help, please talk to me.

Spell-check itself can be a dangerous thing, especially if you use this helpful facility when checking your spelling and grammar and don't fully concentrate. An email or letter can suddenly take on a whole new dimension when it is left to Bill's spell-check mischief: 'Dear John, Yesterday's mating was very reproductive and I enjoyed our firm coming together' or 'Dear Mary, If you could sing the enclosed copy better I will be very fretful.' In today's modern world, be careful with that spell-check – it can be dungarees!

Just as dangerous is predictive texting or predictive email addresses. It is so very easy to send an email to completely the wrong person or say something quite bizarre: 'Hi John, I am at the officialdom new and will sit up the protractor ready for our present. See you in half a house.' It seems technology is no better at predicting the future than we humans.

Email has replaced the traditional office memo and I really mourn those office missives as they always felt so very authoritative, like a message from the headmaster; in other words something to completely ignore. Following the death of the office memo we have filled the vacuum with the glory of the email, but isn't email technology abused in an outrageous way, especially in our working life? Thanks to the Internet we now have the ability to send communications to hundreds of people and do so instantly with very little effort at all, and that's exactly what we do. Instead of sending our email to the two people who actually need to read it, we copy it to a dozen others; instead of reading our draft email carefully and checking what we have said, we send it instantly, gobbledegook and all; instead of putting some effort into our grammar, spelling and structure we use staccato language with the minimum of respect or style: 'Paul … OK … do it … check it though.' It's the language of master to slave and says, 'I'm too busy to spend any time over my communication with you.'

When my wife and I both work at home on the same day, we are nicely set up with links to the office and of course with full Internet access, her in the kitchen or dining room, me in the study. At intervals during the day she is likely to get emails from me saying something like, 'It's your turn to make a cup of tea – any chance of a digestive biscuit?' Now that's what I call progress, saving me walking 15 yards and avoiding any risk of straining my vocal chords.

One of the most dangerous of Microsoft Outlook's features is the Contact Database facility. Using this feature you can 'Send to all' such as to all the sales team or to all the accounting team on the fourth floor. Therefore, when you are about to send an email to 'Sally' in accounts asking her if she might like to go out again tonight on another romantic interlude ('I thought last night was special … Would you like a repeat?'), please be careful that you don't send it to 'Sales' instead of 'Sally'.

On the bright side, emails have certainly enriched my life, as I can't imagine how else I would have discovered the joys of strangers approaching me and suggesting, 'Give her the time of her life tonight' or 'Add an extra 3 inches and become a special man'. Every day I get at least three emails kindly offering to improve me physically; do they know something I don't? I still haven't received an email spam saying, 'See a video of Paris Hilton in her hotel room playing dominoes' or, on a more cultural and sophisticated level, 'Marquetry, the hobby of connoisseurs', but there is always hope.

Emails somehow manage to be both impersonal and private at the same time. Internet chatrooms can be deeply personal and therefore they can be a dangerous form of communication. Because one's communication with others in chatrooms is so personal and connected, extra care is required. It is very easy to inadvertently miscommunicate, because by its nature the chatroom involves fast typing and little thought. How many young girls fall out with their friends just because they didn't take care over what they typed? 'She was my best friend! How could she say that to me? Now I will never talk to her again.'

Quality communication is vital in any relationship and approximately 60 per cent of all the 380,000 homeless people in the UK state a 'dispute with family, friends or partner' as the reason they are on the streets – so this communication business is a serious matter. Communication problems can cause all manner of relationship problems and this is particularly true when men and women communicate with each other. The crux of the problem is that we don't really understand each other and this is a big barrier to smooth, or at least survivable, communication. In a male/female sexual relationship there are dangers at every turn and I suspect that these dangers similarly exist in male/male and female/female relationships where sex rears its ugly head.

Most of these communication minefields start with a conversation and thus beware of words when talking to your sexual partner! There are three 'Lethal Questions' to watch out for and you would be well advised to be on red-alert if you hear any of these questions aimed at you. The first of these is hidden in the form of a plain and simple 'yes' or 'no' style question and it's: 'Do I look fat in this dress?' Let's assume it's a female asking, as if it's not the answer should always be, 'Get out of my dress now! You'll stretch it and I won't be able to wear it again.' It seems the answer to this terrifying question should never be the truth, because that's a 'no-win' answer. Neither are the following answers advisable: 'No you don't, but you carry a little extra weight well' and 'No, it flatters your curves'. The absolutely worst answer might be: 'It depends what you mean by fat.'

The second potentially lethal question is 'Do you love me?' Let's assume you do love him or her, and therefore seemingly the obvious answer is 'Yes, of course I do'. This is where communication becomes so complicated. Simply saying 'yes' implies you haven't taken the question seriously enough and therefore by definition you can't love him or her, otherwise you would have given a more thoughtful response. Adding 'of course I do' devalues the integrity of the 'yes' and therefore this won't do either. Other catastrophic answers include an attempt at reassurance ('I suppose so, it depends what you mean by love'), the whimsical or philosophical ('Love, now isn't it a funny thing?') or the tragic attempt at avoidance ('But do you love me?').

If you do manage to deal with these two questions then beware of the third potentially deathly question and that is 'What would you do if anything happened to me?' The problem with a woman asking this question of her man is that a male automatically goes into problem-solving mode and this will inevitably deliver a poor result for him. Men instantly run ahead in time, straight past the grieving process, imagine being a widower and start thinking of how their life would function on a very practical basis – shocking, I know, but men are genetically preconditioned to do this.

Men would tend to focus upon functional matters such as where the family would live, the financial issues, who would cook meals, how much is the insurance payout and other technical and operational challenges. Because at the moment the question is asked they haven't yet lost their loved one, it is likely a man would find it difficult and indeed terrifying to imagine the depth of emotion they would feel in the event of tragically losing their life partner. This doesn't mean they don't care; it means they can't and don't want to visit these emotions at that moment in time. However, for a man, to answer the question 'What would you do if anything happened to me?' with 'Well, first up I would use the insurance money to build a bigger bathroom, because I think the kids would need this' is, quite simply, tantamount to emotional suicide.

The most dangerous question for a man to ask a woman is 'Are you OK?' This is similar to opening the sluices of the Hoover Dam with him sitting in a rowing boat downstream. The problem is that there is likely to be only two ways this will progress: either things aren't OK and he is likely to be in receipt of a significant dose of responsive emotion – to which he must never offer solutions; or things are very OK and the immediate response will be 'Why do you ask? Aren't things OK with you?' Either way life will have become less simple, productive and happy for both parties and just because one of them asked the wrong question.

The obvious solution is not to use words at all when communicating. There are plenty of alternative methodologies such as grunting, sighing, laughing (preferably together, not at each other), whistling (indicating all is well), humming, groaning (always a favourite), snoring (more on this later) and, not to be recommended even if you liked the meal, burping.

Abdicating all forms of spoken communication is clearly not the answer and would definitely not be supported by Relate. Most experts on human communication encourage us to learn the art of listening, which is sound, although challenging, advice. Let's start our journey into the unknown by exploring different ways to hear those three potentially lethal questions we considered earlier.

Perhaps if a woman asks 'Do I look fat in this dress?' she means, 'I'm feeling a little insecure about how I look. Please just listen and show me you care how I feel, as I don't need you to do or solve anything for me.' This constitutes many more words than the seven words of the actual question, but can you imagine how much better things would develop if men heard this question instead?

'Do you love me?' probably means, 'You haven't said you love me for a while. Please don't forget to reassure me from time to time.' 'What would you do if anything happened to me?' probably simply means, 'Would you miss me dreadfully if I wasn't here' (deceased or otherwise). If you hear the correct question, then the correct answer is so much more straightforward, or so they say!

One centre of so-called excellence where the people are studiously trained in the art of communication is the modern phenomenon of call centres. In the case of telesales call centres, some would suggest their staff are trained in the art of 'not listening'.

However, I almost prefer the Delhi-based technical support

centre to the emotional torture that you endure during a journey through an automated telephone system. You call in to speak to a support person regarding your forthcoming holiday because you have a specific question that isn't covered on their website and immediately the torture starts. 'Press 1 if you would like to book a flight'; 'Press 2 if you want to book a packaged holiday'; 'Press 3 if you want to pay the balance of your holiday'; 'Press 4 if you want to know about airport car parking'; 'Press 5 if you want to request special menus'; 'Press 6 if you want to hear the list again.' You immediately go into panic mode and think to yourself, 'Is there no button to actually speak to a human being?' You realise that you need an alternative strategy and you think, 'Well, if I trick them by pressing the wrong button and then deviously get through to a human being, I can ask that individual to put me through to the right person to then ask my question.' Crafty old me!

You start again by pressing 1 and then get offered a brand-new menu; 'Press 1 if you are flying to the USA'; 'Press 2 if you are travelling to Europe'; 'Press 3 if you are travelling anywhere else'; 'Press 4 if you want to hear the list again.' You cheat again and press 1 and then to your horror hear: 'Press 1 if you want to confirm your passport details'; 'Press 2 if you want to make a new reservation'; 'Press 3 if you want to change an existing reservation' and, you will know this by heart now, 'Press 4 if you want to hear the list again.' At times like this it helps your blood pressure to think of how lonely old people could spend whole afternoons looping through the menus of these automated systems just to have some company.

When your cheating ploy works and you actually get to speak to a breathing human being who works in 'Flight Sales USA', you explain you need to speak to someone about your change of name issue and they are very pleasant. They tell you that you have called the wrong department (of course you know this really and you feel suitably smug having beaten the system) and they offer to put you through to the correct person. All seems well and you hear the phone ringing continuously, find yourself becoming excited about the prospect of speaking to the right person, until the call is answered and then you hear, 'Press 1 if you want to confirm your passport details'; 'Press 2 if you want to learn about marquetry' … Your spirit is broken and they have won. You see you can't beat the system. Your consolation comes from knowing that the travel company will be saving lots of money by using this automated system, unless of course they so frustrate customers as to ensure they never return.

If you email them it isn't much better either. If you are flying out of the country in three days and need an answer to a simple question, then, because email is the most efficient method of modern communication, that's what you send. You dutifully send your email query by clicking on the email support link which is carefully and lovingly provided for you on their website. Almost within minutes you see a reply from Customer Service in your inbox. You think to yourself, 'Now that's what I call efficient.' However, when you open your email it says, 'We thank you for your email. All our customers are important to us and a customer service representative will respond to your email in full within 14 days.' But you will have gone and come back by then! You realise resistance is futile because, you see, you can't halt progress.

Another area where technology is rapidly changing methods of communication is Facebook. In fact, things are moving so fast that the Queen was even shown Facebook on a mobile phone while officially visiting Vodaphone's UK headquarters in November 2008, presumably in order that she could check out her mates' holiday photos from the Caribbean! The newspapers are very quick to jump on the anti-Facebook bandwagon and just such an occasion was in May 2009 following an Ohio State University study of 219 students which found that there was some correlation between Facebook usage and lower student grades. However, this was only an exploratory study and yet it was very interesting how newspapers around the world jumped upon this with headlines like 'Social

Websites Harm a Child's Brain' or 'Facebook Fixation Harms Students' Grades'. Quite clearly further comprehensive research is necessary as there are some obvious dangers in how these sites might affect people's behaviours, but it could be too late already.

However, one can see the benefits of Internet socialising, especially for shy teenagers stuck alone in their room, not understood by their parents, unsure of life and who they really are, but at least able to communicate in some form with their peers. As long as it's secure and not a haven for paedophiles, I'm sure it helps teenagers and people of all ages socialise, albeit on a virtual basis. If virtual contact replaces real-life contact then I'm sure the quality of life is diluted but if it opens doors for real-life contact then it must enrich many a person's life.

In times long since past, people communicated with each other in a quaint way which we called handwritten letters. Jane Austen would write long flowing beautifully crafted and well-versed letters to her friends. However, Jane Austen was an exception and the vast majority of people in these times were not sufficiently educated to write a letter and the mail would have taken much longer than today to reach its destination, except of course when we have a strike! At least nowadays communication is available to us all and the word on the street is that it's instant.

When it comes to communication, words are valuable things. The average tabloid newspaper uses approximately 8,000 different words in each edition and Scrabble lists 160,000 words of nine letters or less. The average pocket-sized English dictionary includes approximately 100,000 words and most people know (but do not necessarily use) an amazing 30,000 words. Therefore, there is clearly plenty of choice for us all to say what we want to say, if only we knew what we wanted to say.

The English language has the most words of any language and the total is estimated at over one million words. Don't be too daunted by this gigantic statistic as it has been suggested that by knowing just 2,000 English words one could understand enough of the language to communicate at a reasonable, if basic, level. An average child aged five will already know between 2,500 and 5,000 words and once at school they learn about 3,000 new words a year. The human brain is indeed a mighty computer.

Despite all this choice and our enormous human brain capacity we still manage to make a mess of inter-gender communication. We started this chapter on the importance of listening rather than speaking and it seems apt that a chapter dealing with communication should finish with a reaffirmation of the importance of what one hears, as opposed to the words one speaks. Men really are simple creatures and women would be well advised to remember this in their communication with the male of the species. Some British men's basic needs are simple and drive them through life, some might say blindly. They are of course what we might call the 'Three Fs', these being Food, Sex (work this out for yourself) and Football. When you hear your man say 'Let's have a nice night in', he doesn't mean 'I would love to enjoy a nice cosy night in together'; he means 'There is a game on at 8 p.m. and would you let me watch it?' When he says, 'Are you hungry?' he means, 'Could you make me a sandwich, please?' and, of course, when he says 'Would you like to go out for a romantic dinner?' he means 'Can we eat and then have sex?' Men!

Our idealistic desire for effective communication is unfortunately often undermined by one of our basic instincts and that is for both men and women to enjoy themselves, which brings us suitably to the next subject: food and drink.

17

Eat, Drink and Be Merry

Human beings need some things just to survive. Food and drink are two of these essentials, with merriment being a bonus. With our TVs now full of survival programmes, many of us are now well versed in the key survival requirements and thanks to Ray Mears and Bear Grylls, a lot of people now know the order of priority for survival, which is of course: shelter, then fresh clean water, and finally food.

It is generally recognised that going without water for just one day is a very dangerous situation to be in. Water lost through perspiration and breathing needs to be replaced and the normal guide is a minimum of two quarts of water a day. Retaining liquids is vital but what I haven't seen on TV survival programmes is a requirement to top up with ten pints of Stella, a litre of Chardonnay or a dozen tequila shots.

Let's start by being honest. It has to be said that eating is an enjoyable experience, isn't it? Equally true is the fact that many of us eat far too much, or too much of what we shouldn't. Survival experts say that when our body is starved of food we become irritable, lethargic, weak, disoriented, demoralised and our immune systems weakened, and none of these are good things. Unfortunately, many of us have spent our whole life dedicated to avoiding these symptoms – and probably too dedicated.

The reality is that the human body can survive for a long period of time without food. Doctors say the body can survive up to about 42 days without food and hunger strikers often live for more than 60 days without sustenance. Each pound of fat contains over 3,500 calories which is about one and a half day's normal intake and, as we now know, this would become quite handy if marooned at sea for any length of time (see Chapter 2).

The modern trend for more and more survival reality TV shows might just explain the parallel rise in the popularity of cookery shows. We now have a whole range of cookery reality shows such as *Masterchef* and *Come Dine with Me*, plus the traditional educational cookery shows featuring those too numerous to mention celebrity chefs, or the participation shows like Gordon 'F' Ramsay's. This is a far cry from the groundbreaking cookery shows of Fanny Craddock, the Galloping Gourmet and, of course, the late and great Keith Floyd, with his liquid slant on things.

Today the options for meal choices are enormous with a huge range of different menu types to help stack up those 3,500 calories. We have Mexican, Indian, Chinese, Thai, Vietnamese, American Diner, French, Italian, Spanish, Moroccan, Goan, Argentinian, Traditional English, but strangely no Australian. A win for the Poms, but to be fair this isn't strictly a true result. In fact, our Oz cousins get little or no credit for one of our now great British culinary institutions, the 'Barbie Queue' (curses again to that spell-check).

As far as I'm concerned, BBQs were an Australian invention and of course Ken's immortal food-fetish cry, 'Put another shrimp on my Barbie', epitomises this. My brother lived in Australia for nearly ten years in the 1960s and 1970s and when he returned for a visit in 1976 he introduced us to the wonders of BBQs. It is difficult to imagine now, but back then in the 1970s BBQs were not part of our British summer social scene at all. BBQs in Britain are essentially only 30-odd years old and not even at that doubt-ridden midlife crisis stage. Difficult to imagine, isn't it?

Of course BBQs are great opportunities to sample the delights of singed sausage skins wrapped around raw meat. We even have a government health warning in the form of radio and TV advertisements regarding undercooked BBQ food – so nanny is clearly worried about this! One has to admit that cooking on a charcoal BBQ is not the easiest thing in the world, hampered as one is by, on the one hand, paranoia driven by government adverts about cooking the food properly and, on the other hand, the challenge of not frazzling all the food. In fact, it seems to me that on a traditional charcoal BBQ it is virtually impossible to achieve the required perfect cooking heat for sufficient time to cook the food properly and therefore, as a true government-advised health-and-safety aware citizen, you undertake a comprehensive risk assessment and come to the conclusion that it's less risky to foul up their meal than poison them, so you frazzle the chicken!

Only in Britain could we develop a market for Barbie Queue patio heaters which creates bizarre visions of blonde bimbo dolls waiting in an orderly line to jump on the fire! Most other nations would consider it quite odd to continue sitting outside eating when the temperature is so cold as to make it uncomfortable, and the obvious solution is not to purchase a £300 gas patio heater but to go indoors into the warmth and comfort of your home. Because we get so few genuinely warm balmy evenings and because we so want to be like our exotic Antipodean cousins, we stay outside huddled around the dying embers, just so that we can say we have experienced outdoor living. However, there is hope on the horizon for all those hardcore British outdoor types and that is in the form of global warming, which presumably means Homebase will fill the retail space currently selling patio heaters with sunshades and those grand, deluxe gas BBQs that are really something to show off to your friends.

I have to admit that I love BBQs; I enjoy those lovely English fresh salads with radishes, coleslaw, potato salad and beetroot. I like the wine, I like donning the chef's apron, wielding the tongs and socialising. The trouble is that in most British summers we are only able to have a couple of BBQs owing to the often inclement weather. Unfortunately, as no doubt you have experienced yourself, you normally need to plan such a social event and the bare minimum climatic conditions are that it should be warm enough to sit outside at 8 p.m. and that there should be no rain. We do have a number of summer days like this but not on demand and that's the problem: it's the unpredictability. As a result it's another win for the Aussies: 'Throw another prawn on Ken's girl in celebration.'

In fact, as recently as the 1970s British cuisine was very limited and we hadn't expanded our horizons very far: 'I'm not eating that foreign muck!' Meat, potatoes and two veg was the order of the day and in many ways we owe it to the array of Chinese takeaways that erupted across Britain in the 1970s for our current considerably more cosmopolitan dining culture and probably increased obesity.

How things have changed, although in fact Indian restaurant food isn't actually Indian food at all; it's a British version of an Indian style of cuisine with extra salt, fat, meat and sugar thrown in to appeal to our palates. There is now an estimated annual spend on eateries in the UK of £25 billion with £365 million spent on fast-food establishments and all this change happened in the last 30 years.

Chicken tikka masala is much quoted as Britain's most popular 'dining-out' dish, battering to submission our home-grown fish n' chips. The average chicken tikka masala contains a huge 850 calories and over 45 grams of fat, just in one serving. One chicken tikka masala with pilau rice provides you with five of your six grams of daily salt. Many traditional Indian dishes are vegetarian or contain small amounts of meat or fish, which is very different to the uniquely British version of Indian food. Even a plain piece of naan bread can contain 400 calories, so beware of too many of those Indian takeaways.

However, in my experience the biggest threat from an Indian takeaway is not to the health of your body but to the health of your kitchen worktop. If you spill just a drop of that sauce from any dish on to your work surface and don't wipe it up straight away, that strange yellow colouring takes over like a form of lethal virus. At once it starts to eat into your worktop with its yellow bile and you can't get it off with any kitchen cleaner. In fact, if you use bleach it doesn't touch the stuff at all, but it does take the colour from your worktop. It's vicious stuff.

Why is it that the stain is always yellow, even if the dish wasn't? For some reason the colour of the stain always evolves to that corrosive yellow; fascinating, but what is in these dishes? If it can do this to your hardened and veneered work surface, what does it do to your stomach? Does everyone who has ever had an Indian meal develop a yellow staining to the wall of their stomach lining? When surgeons encounter this during incisions, they must say, 'I see, another Indian takeaway connoisseur.'

Despite this, one has to admit that Indian restaurant food in Britain, albeit adapted to our Western taste buds, is very tasty and you can see why it is so popular. If you are really hungry then there just isn't a better way to fill your stomach. A good lamb pasanda, pilau rice and an onion bhaji will do the job nicely. In fact, wash it down with a couple of pints of lager and you will not want sustenance of any kind for at least 36 hours. Have you noticed how Indian food seems to reduce your appetite to nil over the next day? Is it that mysterious yellow colouring expanding when it meets your stomach juices?

On the other hand, as we all know, a Chinese takeaway has exactly the opposite effect. Straight after a feast of prawn crackers, sweet-and-sour chicken and egg-fried rice, you feel bloated and unable to eat another mouthful. However, give it a couple of hours and the hunger pangs return, usually accompanied by a raging thirst. Chinese takeaway food doesn't have that mysterious yellow liquid but many dishes do seem to frequently include a brown liquid with that strange tactile consistency, which thankfully doesn't stain the worktop. All this appears to confirm my theory that it's the colouring that affects our bodily responses.

However, don't worry as we have the government to look after us. The UK Food Standards Agency was set up, amongst other things, to protect us from health hazards in food. According to the Food Standards Agency, E249 and E252 are vital to prevent bacteria in food stuffs such as cured meats, bacon and corned beef. The specific legislation covering preservatives is the Miscellaneous Food Additives Regulations 1995, SI 1995 No. 3187 as amended by SI 1997 No. 1413, SI 1999 No. 1136, SI 2001 No. 60, SI 2001 No. 3775 and many more.

Of course, preservatives are necessary, as without them much of our food would perish before it even got to the supermarket shelf.

This is reassuring until you look into the extent of the E numbers and it's quite frankly worrying. E numbers can be placed into eight groups: preservatives, antioxidants, sweeteners, emulsifiers, stabilisers, thickeners, gelling agents and 'others'. The group of 'others' is made up of acid, acidity regulators, anti-caking agents, anti-foaming agents, bulking agents, carriers and carrier solvents, emulsifying salts, firming agents, flavour enhancers, flour treatment agents, foaming agents, glazing agents, humectants, modified starches, packaging gases, propellants, raising agents and sequestrants. It doesn't sound very appetising and 'packaging gases' sound particularly unappealing.

We range from E100 to over E1500 now and the list is growing. Each E number sounds so unappetising and an example from each group exemplifies this: E140 are chlorophylls and chlorophyllins, not to put you to sleep but a colouring; E251 is sodium nitrate, not an explosive but a preservative; E321 is butylated hydroxytoluene, not tampered-with hair colouring but an antioxidant; and E966 is lactitol, not to help you clear your bowels but a sweetener.

However, we mustn't concern ourselves too much because our legislators have all this in hand and food labels are required by law to show: volume or weight, date mark and ingredients with percentages. More worrying, however, is what the legislation doesn't require and it is these loopholes that food producers so cleverly use to their advantage. Examples are the marketing 'power words' that potentially confuse us: farmhouse, wholesome and traditional, all of which mean nothing and have no legal definition at all. Clever, isn't it? They don't have to be particularly accurate with country of origin either which means British bacon can be made from Danish bacon but cured in the UK – it is where the food last underwent substantial change that matters. Confusing, isn't it? There is no requirement for nutritional information as this only has to be given if other claims are made such as low salt. They can use imprecise health claims and low fat doesn't necessarily mean low sugar, which may well have been added to offset the taste impact of the low fat content. They are legally able to indicate potentially misleading content: smoked haddock could mean soaked in a smoke-flavour solution rather than lovingly smoked over bark for three days in the Highlands. It's not really what you would expect. Often our food is not what it seems, so be aware.

Life has certainly changed over the years and when I was a boy, one of my mother's daily activities was food shopping. She would walk a mile to the local stores in the morning to buy that evening's meal for her family from, first, the local butcher (fresh locally produced meat), the greengrocer (fruit and vegetables in season), the baker (freshly baked on-site bread for the morning's breakfast) and then to the local store for the little extras like Oxo as recommended by the TV Oxo mum and Fairy Liquid ('Hands that do dishes can be soft as your face'). It was a daily routine that ensured a number of things: her family ate wholesome fresh food, she was kept occupied during the day and as a bonus she maintained a high level of fitness.

We also had a large garden in our country council house and my dad converted both sides of the garden into a huge vegetable plot, or more accurately a mini allotment. Probably only those of my generation, or perhaps today's generation who have gone retro with fresh food, will remember or know the beautiful flavour of vegetables picked or dug up from the garden that morning, and then brought freshly prepared and cooked straight to your plate. In fact, you could argue that some vegetables taste so different when cooked this fresh that they are difficult to recognise as being the same botanical species as their normal supermarket counterparts. New potatoes are one of these; runner beans, cabbages, carrots ... in fact most vegetables. There is one exception and these are peas which, strangely, seem to taste much better in the frozen form, as opposed to fresh from the pods. I checked a bag of frozen peas and could find no reference to added sugar or salt or E1105 and so, in this case at least, I'm reassured.

This rose-tinted nostalgia doesn't really tell the whole story, as

I'm sure my mother became very frustrated by this mundane daily chore, but once I left primary school things changed. The world started to change and people wanted more than this kind of simple life; they wanted cars, holidays and electronic gadgets like the colour TVs that were starting to become available. The only way to pay for all these little extras was for the wife to work as well as the husband and so they did. Because the rest of society were on a similar path, food producers started to offer ready-made meals like those already on offer in America (where they were called TV dinners) and life changed for good ... or not, as the case may be.

With my mum and many of her peers working, convenience was the order of the day and this opened the way for the rise and rise of the supermarkets to their current illustrious position where they now rule the retail world. As you know, supermarkets now sell virtually anything to anyone and their premise seems to be: 'Once you are in, we'll work on you to increase customer spend.'

The 'Big Four' of Tesco, Asda, Sainsbury's and Morrisons now account for approximately three-quarters of the UK grocery market. There is an uncanny parallel with football's 'Big Four' where Tesco might be Manchester United and Asda could be Chelsea, Sainsbury's Arsenal and Morrisons Liverpool. Are the Co-operative Group really Aston Villa and Waitrose really Manchester City? If only Marks and Spencer were Southampton FC.

However, it hasn't all been plain sailing for the supermarkets, as a number of well-known chains no longer exist and most have been gobbled up by the bigger boys. Do you remember any of this list: Alldays, Bejam, Carrefour, David Greig, Fine Fare, Galbraith's, Hinton's, Kwik Save, Safeway, and Supernational? In fact, Hinton's history of being bought by the Argyll Group for their Presto chain, to then become Safeway and finally to become part of Morrisons, highlights the nature of the most recent history of this retail market.

The largest UK supermarket is Tesco plc who at the time of writing employed around 300,000 staff in over 2,200 stores in

Britain, as well as a further 2,100 stores in China, the Czech Republic, Hungary, India, Japan, Malaysia, Poland, Republic of Ireland, Slovakia, South Korea, Thailand, Turkey and the USA. The number of UK employees roughly equals the population of Southampton. Tesco's results released in April 2010 show a mammoth sales revenue figure of approximately £62.5 billion and so it seems it's true: every little helps.

The record reported profits were £3.4 billion, larger than some countries' GDPs – for example those of Luxembourg, Paraguay and Jamaica – but, thank goodness, not Kazakhstan, or heaven knows what the suicide rate would be there! Tesco's sales revenue is nearly half the GDP of a great country like New Zealand, so next up then, it has to be a Tesco rugby team.

Supermarkets now sell huge quantities of alcohol and this would really be useful if Tesco did start their own rugby team. In our modern world, excess alcohol consumption is becoming an increasing problem, as we seem to have gone from enjoyable social drinking to hard-core binge drinking in just one generation. The number of alcohol-related deaths in the UK is surprisingly low, with the National Statistics Office reporting 8,724 such deaths in 2007. Doctors believe the longer-term impact of excessive drinking in people's younger years is yet to truly affect these statistics. Many of these alcohol-related deaths are on the road where approximately 3,000 people are killed or seriously injured each year. In 2004 Fife Police force ran a profiling exercise of people found over the limit when in charge of a car. They found that 85 per cent of drivers were male, almost half were aged 17 to 30 and the majority were employed. Most worrying was the fact that 54 per cent of them knew the penalties for drink driving and 87 per cent had no intention of drinking and driving earlier that day. This really highlights the mindset of someone acting in a different way with alcohol in their body, as opposed to when they are sober.

If you do get stopped by the police and you have foolishly been drinking, there are some specific words that are best avoided, as they really do give the game away. Therefore, in this situation you would be well advised never to try to be clever with your oratory abilities, just to show off your sobriety: 'Officer, I feel your less than innovative, constitutionalised intervention tonight will have no substantive effect upon the proliferation of drunk drivers.'

Unfortunately, the problem with being drunk is that good advice falls on deaf ears and regrettably the three phrases you never hear drunk people say are: 'No I don't really fancy a kebab because it's the last thing my body needs now'; 'I am calling it a day now because I need to get up early tomorrow for work'; or finally, 'Where is the nearest public toilet as I refuse to degrade myself and be sick in the street?' But some people never say this when they are the worse for wear. That's the problem with excess drink: we make bad decisions that felt perfect at the time!

Concerns about excess drinking don't just apply to men either. Police statistics released in 2008 showed a 50-per-cent increase in certain parts of Britain over the previous five years in female drunk-and-disorderly arrests, though this is good news for reality shows such as *Brit Cops Zero Tolerance* and *Binge Britain*. The West Midlands and Gwent force had the largest increases – naughty Brummie and Celtic girls! Don Shenker of Alcohol Concern said, 'The trouble is that women's bodies cannot handle these large amounts of alcohol.' Thanks to today's less than delicate female role models, gone are the good old days of buying your girlfriend a couple of Babychams to help loosen her inhibitions; you would need a whole vat of wine today, or so I'm told.

To be fair to today's modern generation there is a much greater awareness of the need to avoid drinking and driving than in, for instance, the 1960s and 1970s. This has led to a new condition which we might call 'Soberseeitclearus', after the Roman god of Strong Lager. This is the symptom you suffer when you are taking medicine and can't drink, or you are the chosen driver for the night, or perhaps you just don't drink and you find yourself in the company of a group of drunken people. Typically, this might be at a party, perhaps where you drive to pick up a friend or loved one and get invited in. Unless you like Soberseeitclearus, say 'No, thank you' and retire gracefully.

People who are merry and full of alcoholic beverages are completely and sometimes charmingly unaware of the change in their behaviour. When we are the worse for wear from drink we talk at 20 decibels louder than is necessary, when we talk to others we get at least 6 inches too close to people's faces (sometimes inadvertently throwing in a little spittle for effect), are certain everything we say is outrageously funny, have a tendency to get angry if people don't agree with us, become philosophers on life and its mysteries and, best of all, 'we love you' and become gushing with our emotions.

When you are drunk all this seems perfectly normal behaviour and everyone goes around a party happily sharing in this and it's called 'having fun'. However, find yourself sober and you will see all this strange behaviour with great clarity, and then you have Soberseeitclearus. If they ever feature this word in a re-energised version of the old TV show *Call My Bluff*, you now know its real meaning.

A special form of alcoholic beverage that is particularly popular in our modern world is the cocktail. The first publication to refer to cocktails is considered to be 1862's *How to Mix Drinks; or, The Bon Vivant's Companion*, or a bartender's guide. In this guide ten popular recipes were referred to as cocktails. The cocktail's origins are subject to many urban myths but my particular favourite is the tale that local bartenders in Campeche, Mexico, used wooden spoons carved from a native root known as *cola de gallo* (cock's tail) to stir the local spirits and punches before serving. My own favourite is the margarita; traditionally served on ice with salt rubbed around the rim. Cocktail:uk, an online specialist website, lists its ten most popular cocktails and I wager they have little similarity at all to good old *Bon Vivant's Companion's* top ten.

Today's top ten are, as is the usual practice, announced in reverse order. Last, at number 10, but not least is the Screaming Orgasm (multiple orders receive discounts), followed by the Margarita (hooray), Sex on the Beach (a bit of grit never harmed anyone), Dry Martini (shaken not stirred, still hanging in there), Mojito (exotic fun), Virgin Pussy (no comment), Cosmopolitan (I will try any mixture), Porn Star (this drink lasts all night) and the winner at number one is simply called Sex. Have you noticed how five of the ten most popular cocktails have sensual connotations, which confirms yet again our subconscious linkage between a good time and sex?

Events to celebrate special occasions are always fun and it is very pleasant to mix with friends, family and loved ones in a convivial friendly atmosphere. Most important occasions now have an array of websites to help plan, organise or book a very special evening or, more than likely, day or weekend. Pre-wedding stag celebrations used to be called stag nights but in keeping with our trend towards excess, we now have stag weekends and even stag weeks. No doubt the economies of Dublin, Las Vegas, Prague and Edinburgh thrive on these events although I'm not sure how much it adds to the cultural value of those living in these beautiful cities (Las Vegas excluded).

A favourite celebration party is a wedding reception. These are typically very happy events with two people who love each other reaffirming their mutual commitment to each other and to go to Relate if things get tough. The feast of lukewarm food is over, much wine is drunk, toasts are complete, tears of joy have been shed, everyone has laughed at the best man's speech (except the mother-in-law) and it's time for the disco.

This is the time for fun and, with everyone happy, relaxed and slightly tipsy, all is set for an evening of fun. We have the couple's first dance, Dad dancing with his daughter, the bride, music for all tastes and of course the ritual of dancing to YMCA. The evening ends when the music licence runs out, the DJ packs up and everyone retires to their bedroom to reflect on a great day and enjoy a private 'Cocktail Number 10' with their loved one!

Common sense says that too much drink is obviously bad for you, although as with all things in life, moderation is the answer, which brings us suitably to the next subject: health and well-being.

18

Live Long and Prosper

We have already considered the lifelong burden of taxes and now it's time to reflect upon the other certainty in life and that is, perversely, death; and, more importantly, how we can stave off its arrival as long as possible.

The quality of our life is directly affected by our health or, more accurately, it is reduced if we don't have good health. Health is one of those things in life where there is no upside, just a downside. If you have good health, you probably take it for granted (score nought) and if you don't have good health it probably adversely affects the quality of your life (you get a minus). If we just realised how lucky we were when we have good health, it would add so much to the quality of our life (our score would be plus one).

The World Health Organisation (WHO) defines health as 'A state of complex physical, mental and social well-being and not merely the absence of disease or infirmity.' To achieve good health, it is said that the following factors need to be in place: good nutrition, exercise, hygiene, a positive social environment and supportive stress-free conditions. Oh dear, this sounds challenging. Help!

As a race, and contrary to media deliverances, the reality is that the British are doing fairly well in terms of our health. According to the National Statistics Office in 2007, male life expectancy has risen by five and a half years over the last 25 years, to stand at an average of 77.2 years and this continues to rise. To gain some perspective on this subject, at the turn of the twentieth century life expectancy for men was only 45 years. This is a staggering increase of 70 per cent over about four generations and something of which as a race we should feel proud, although strangely we don't.

Craftily, women seem to outlive men by 4.3 years, but this gap is coming down, so watch out, ladies! There are also some strange regional anomalies: life expectancy for women in the south-west of England is 82.9 years but 80.4 in the north-east. The obvious conclusion, with women living longer than men is that if you are a macho male Newcastle United supporter, there are three things you must do to increase your chances of living a longer life: first, move to Devon immediately; second, take the plunge and have that sex change operation and, third (and much worse for a Geordie than a sex change operation), start supporting Manchester United (less stress).

The answer to longevity isn't to take flight to the beautiful Pacific as male life expectancy in the Philippines is only 64 years, so surprisingly it makes logical sense to move from Manila to Middlesbrough. The WHO report from its Commission on the Social Determinants of Health showed that social and environmental conditions, much more than genetics, are the key factors affecting health and life expectancy. It found that a child born in the Glasgow suburb of Calton will live on average a staggering 28 years less than a boy born in its close affluent neighbour, Lenzie.

The magazine *Forbes* examined some key factors such as air pollution, drinking water quality, infant mortality, illness, nourishment rates and life expectancies to create a list of the world's healthiest countries. The less-than-surprising result was that the fresh air and socially developed cultures of Iceland, Sweden and Finland easily made up the top three. Frighteningly, the UK didn't make the first 15. Our big rival, Australia, came in at sixth and, for all their alleged obesity, the Americans came in at 11th. For all that, I have yet to find a country around the world I would rather live in than our green and pleasant land, but to be fair I don't live in a British inner city!

A country's net growth in population is determined by its birth rate and its inhabitants' average life expectancy. This net growth represents a fine balance between the two and as a result we have the crazy situation where some countries like Italy and Malaysia are encouraging their citizens to mate, while others, controversially China with its 'one child' policy, are discouraging them. In the 1960s the Australian government's £10 immigration incentive to UK residents was one way of rectifying population imbalances. Don't fret too much on behalf of the Italian and Malaysian governments because the good news for them is that sex is not a particularly unpleasant human experience and thus all should soon be well. As a result of this magical human design we don't do that badly with procreation and, as at 2007, the world birth rate was 20 babies per 1,000 head of population and this means 134 million babies a year are born around the world and I think a big 'well done' to our Creator is in order here.

The good news is that this keeps midwives in a job and they deserve it too. Midwifery is an ancient profession; there are records of midwives (or their equivalents) in ancient Egypt from 1500 BC. In antiquity it was believed having the mother stand upright helped with the birth, whereas of course today methodologies such as water births are the vogue. In medieval times the Church became involved in midwifery as they were concerned about witchcraft. The Church required midwives to be licensed by a bishop and swear an oath not to use magic, whereas of course today all they have to do is have professional indemnity insurance.

In fact, two of the most human and of course humane of jobs must be those of midwives and undertakers. Working in these two ancient professions one must get a real perspective on life; through death one can appreciate life and only through birth can one truly appreciate the wonder of life. This is all very well but today you do often hear midwives complain of overwork and the stress of their job, though isn't that the case with every job nowadays in our efficiency-conscious Britain?

Undertakers do a wonderful job but one of the skills that I believe they don't get credit for is as after-dinner speakers. They have fabulous black stories to tell but their best attributes are a well-balanced view of life and a tremendous sense of humour. I love the way they seem to respect grieving families' emotional needs, show great sensitivity and yet don't take life too seriously. How else could they survive the strong emotions involved in their profession?

Therapists often refer to the Kübler-Ross Model that says there are five stages of grieving: denial (which acts as a kind of protection), anger (at the unfairness of it all), bargaining (attempting to rewrite things), depression (numbness and sadness) and eventually acceptance (the best place to be). People don't necessarily visit every stage or in that order but clearly acceptance is the aim, as, once there, one can still have warm, loving memories of the deceased and return to a productive life. The Irish may have had the answer to getting through these grieving phases as quickly as possible in the form of the wake. This way of saying farewell seems to provide a fast-track through these five phases and I'm not sure why this ritual or even a modern equivalent is apparently retreating into history.

No one wants to die and as a result we quite understandably are acutely aware of the dangers in life – well, if you listen to the media you are! We are constantly being warned of these often imagined or exaggerated dangers, and, in the middle of the June 2009 'deadly heatwave' (an exaggeration, as we saw in Chapter 2), the breakfast news programme ran a slot called '10 Ways to Survive the Heatwave'. Please give me strength. One way to survive was quite simply to turn off your TV and wait for it to rain, which, of course, as you know, it did, a lot and for the rest of the summer.

There are many real dangers in life and one of these dangers appears eating Greek fast-food in Wolverhampton. The BBC reported that a kebab shop owner in 2008 prepared food (if that is what kebabs are) while a co-employee's corpse lay nearby. Needless to say the establishment was closed down but not before this priceless quote from the attending police officer: 'Upon arrival I identified a dead male lying on a sofa at the rear of the main kitchen.' No onions or chilli sauce, thank you!

Another less obvious danger to our health is that of a fridge magnet, or more accurately when one has a heart pacemaker and is in the vicinity of a fridge magnet. The University of Zurich tested the effect of neodymium magnets on 70 heart patients. Close contact within three centimetres is apparently enough to destabilise heart pacemakers. The Swiss researchers suggest manufacturers include a health warning on their products and the obvious solution

199

is a warning fridge magnet that says: 'Please don't be a fridge-picker / That's if you've got a dodgy ticker. / Please beware, my friend, this magnetic message / Might make you even sicker!' None of the quirkiness of the fridge magnet is lost and the important health warning is in place. Cools your heart, doesn't it?

One of the dangers that the government is very keen to remind us all about is that of obesity. There is no doubt that British people are heavier than we ever have been – or some of us are. However, the UK government's obsession with BMI (not British Midland International Airlines but Body Mass Index), which is the comparison between a person's weight and height, probably doesn't help things. The World Health Organisation say waist size is a more accurate measurement as BMI does not take into account gender, muscle or bone structure. According to the *BBC Magazine*, if one uses the BMI measurement in a certain way George Clooney, Brad Pitt and Matt Damon are all potentially obese; nasty fatties! It is true that on average men are approximately half a stone heavier than they were in 1993, but equally we are all living longer, and what a conundrum this is for the government's self-appointed nanny role.

This is the problem with having a 'Nanny State': everything gets exaggerated and as a result we really live in a 'Boy that Cried Wolf State'. As we know, one week we are told that a particular thing will kill us and a few months later we are told the very same thing is good for us. Just such an example was the report in 2006 from the *European Journal of Clinical Nutrition* that dispelled the common belief that tea was 'bad for you' and didn't hydrate. Public health nutritionist Dr Carrie Ruxton of King's College London found clear evidence that drinking four cups of tea a day can cut the chances of having a heart attack, strengthen your bones as well as protect against tooth plaque. After years of being told not to drink tea and only drink water, now we are told drinking tea is good for you. It's all very confusing and worrying I know, but why not relax, sit down and 'Have a nice cup of tea, dear?'

Another example of this type of advice is from Duke University, North Carolina, which said there is evidence that people who eat a curry meal two or three times a week have a lower risk of dementia. Apparently the curcumin in a curry may prevent the spread of amyloid protein plaques, which cause dementia. Therefore, it seems we now have a clear choice between saving our memory and saving our kitchen worktop. Once you make the choice, then all you have to do is remember what you decided!

All this advice can make you paranoid about health and I experienced the unpleasant results of such paranoia when once on my own in Phoenix, Arizona. Just prior to a business trip to the USA I spoke to a friend who had previously suffered deep-vein thrombosis (DVT) and he advised me to 'be careful' when on my travels. Despite this, I foolishly sat all ten hours to Phoenix in economy class, being immersed in a business book that I was writing at the time. I woke the next morning to find my left calf was very tight and sore. I left it 24 hours but the next day the soreness was even worse. Given the advice I had received to 'be careful'; I felt I should do something, so I surfed the Net for advice on DVT. To my horror, when I found a site listing the 'Top 10 DVT Symptoms' I was able to tick off at least six of these symptoms. In panic I spoke to the hotel receptionist who recommended I called the local hospital helpline and of course when I told them of my pre-ordained six symptoms they ordered me into the hospital, immediately and without fail. 'Help, I'm dying!'

Thus I found myself in downtown Phoenix Trauma 1 Hospital to spend one of the worst days of my life. I was on my own, in the American equivalent of A&E, downtown in a big inner city with some less than savoury co-patients, and I was very frightened of dying, not so much from DVT but from my liaison with Phoenix's injured gang members. Needless to say, once I eventually made it to the doctor, the scan revealed no problem other than a strain from my gym work three days earlier; I was relieved and my insurance company was $2,000 worse off. This highlights the dangers of health paranoia, but you won't get any advice from me on this.

One of the most dangerous places in Britain is in fact surprisingly sleepy old Coronation Street. This little Lancastrian street of probably no more than about three dozen houses has been the centre of extensive tragedy and death. Since Steve Tanner's murder on 28 September 1969 there have been 16 murders, which I make one every 2.5 years. On top of this there have been 27 deaths by accident and 4 suicides which I believe means Corrie is a very dungarees (Bill!) place.

One enormous reassurance is to know that all around the world there are scientists working away to help us live more fulfilling and healthy lives by uncovering all manner of enlightening insights. The Ig Nobel Prize each year rewards just such efforts and in 2004 the award for public health went to Jillian Clarke of the Chicago High School for Agricultural Sciences and the Howard University for their investigation into the scientific validity of the 'five second rule', about whether it's safe to eat food that's been dropped on the floor. Tonight you can be at peace in your bed knowing that our health is in good hands or more accurately in Murphy's hands.

Self-image is the greatest gift, or it can be the most extreme torture tool, and like all weapons it's whose hand it's in that determines the result. Unfortunately, the media have such a strong influence over our perceptions of what is good and what is bad that for many people the torture option usually wins. In the 1950s the commonly held perception was that curves were attractive and natural, and this represented beauty in a woman. Today the magazine-driven perception of beauty is just the opposite. Models are normally size-zero stick insects and, as a result, young girls consider themselves fat if they are a size 12. The modern terminology of referring to sizes is arbitrary and takes no account of body structure and cleverly implies that size that is substance is bad, unless of course we see things differently.

Could there be more different beautiful female role models than the curvy size-16 Marilyn Monroe and the modern Keira

Knightley? Consider this: in the early, pre-Twiggy 1960s a thin teenage girl would avoid all eye contact with shop windows, just because she didn't come up to scratch with Marilyn Monroe's, Jayne Mansfield's and Diana Dors' curvy images. Today the size-16 teenage girl avoids all eye contact with those very same shop windows, just because she doesn't look like Posh Spice.

Fashions change, but beauty still remains in the eye of the beholder and a sound, positive and helpful belief is that no one is ugly and there is someone for everyone. This is just my opinion but surely it's worth exploring. Despite this, I suspect we will have more of the controversies such as the BBC's less-than-model-like pre-senter Clare Balding urging the 2009 Grand National-winning jockey Liam Treadwell live on air to 'get his teeth done'. She and the BBC have subsequently apologised for this remark, but the point is that, in our modern designer world, anything less than perfection is considered to need attention. We have a whole chapter later in the book on happiness, but I'm fairly certain true happiness isn't having the best cosmetic surgeon.

One way to look good or more accurately look fitter is to join a gym. Actually it's not, as you need not just to join and pay a gym subscription but then to attend regularly. I couldn't find any statis-tics for the percentage of non-attending gym members as under-standably health clubs want to keep this figure quiet. However, there are now approximately 2.2 million people in the UK who are members of clubs and there are approximately 5,700 clubs. I have a hunch a lot of members don't attend but know they should, although of course in January each year this is a different matter, when the car parks are full with people driven on by their latest New Year's resolution. I have noticed that by February it's back to normal in the car park. Health club subscriptions appear to be the modern equivalent of *Reader's Digest* subscriptions; you know you should, but ...

However, exercise isn't always good for you, as recent research has shown. A Spanish study by the University of Cordoba Medical

School studied top triathletes and found their sperm count to be at only 4 per cent, whereas the normal count is between 15 per cent and 20 per cent. The scientists believe this is due to the overheating of the testicles from tight speedos and the obvious rubbing on the saddle, although on the bright side if you are a randy cyclist trying for a baby you would at least need to have sex four times more frequently to conceive, although, if you are cycling that much, you probably wouldn't have the time or energy anyway.

In our nanny state there is always plenty of advice on offer and an array of things to worry about. It's little surprise then that one of our major health issues is stress. The International Stress Management Association found that more than one in two people suffered from stress once in the preceding year. The TUC estimates that work-related stress costs the economy £7 million per annum and according to the Health and Safety Executive (HSE) an estimated 12.8 million days are lost each year through stress, which understandably must make the HSE quite stressed.

As far as I can recall, until the 1980s stress didn't exist, so it must be a modern virus, but a problem it certainly is, because the HSE has issued a whole helpful guide entitled 'Dealing with Stress'. In this guide the HSE defines stress as 'Not an illness but the adverse reaction people have to excessive pressures or other types of demand placed on them.' I don't completely agree with this, as surely stress is simply feeling out of control, and for us human beings that's very unpleasant. Lots of things can generate an environment where we feel out of control: relationship problems (not enough snow), financial worries (this works every time), worries about job security (currently very relevant), and pressure at work (doing two people's jobs for one wage). Other stress-causing situations might be the absence of a dominoes set in your hotel room, worrying about how much you can sell your next baby picture for or, the ultimate test, a tough marquetry session.

Life's pressures are only ever a step away, whoever you are and whatever your wealth, because feeling out of control is a universal danger. The biggest challenge is to 'not feel out of control' because you are worried about 'feeling out of control'. You must have known someone who gets worried this way! The HSE warns that stress can result in: finding it hard to sleep, changing eating habits, smoking or drinking more, avoiding friends and family, or experiencing sexual problems. They also warn of: tiredness, indigestion, nausea, headaches, aching muscles, palpitations, indecision, lack of concentration, memory loss, feeling inadequate, low self-esteem, anger, irritation, anxiety, feeling numb, hypersensitivity and feeling drained and listless. This in itself is a worrying list.

The HSE helpfully highlights certain symptoms to watch out for and these are their 'nine warning signs': eating on the run, drinking excessively, rushing around, being available to everyone, doing several jobs at once, missing breaks, taking work home, not having enough time for exercise and no time for relaxation in the working day. Sounds like a normal day to me. How did you do? I scored eight out of nine.

Isn't that the problem? In today's computerised, speed-obsessed modern world, the only way to feel in control is either to abdicate and become a latter-day hermit or to plan and manage your life so at least you *feel* you have choice and thus magically feel in control – heaven!

Therapists often talk of some of the more stressful events in life as being divorce, death and burglary (not committing one but suffering one). However, two less obvious potentially stressful events are holidays and the Christmas season (see Chapters 6 and 14). Neil Shah, director of the Stress Management Society, has said, 'No wonder that one in twenty people consider Christmas more stressful than divorce or burglary.'

Surveys of the most stressful careers throw up (through excess anxiety no doubt) the obvious candidates such as prison officers, school teachers and police officers. However, two less typical stressful candidates are head chefs and slaughterers. The least stressful jobs include postmen, hairdressers and, one surprise, speech therapists; you see, it does help to talk! If further evidence was needed, Saqib Saddiq's presentation to the British Psychological Society conference in 2006 seals the case. His study showed that working in a library is the UK's most stressful job. Shussssh!

What can we do about all this potentially harmful stress? One solution is to live by the sea as a poll of 2,000 adults by Hoegaarden found that 84 per cent of people said being in contact with the natural elements made them feel instantly more relaxed and, of these, 42 per cent said the sound of the sea worked best. Just 19 per cent of those people who lived in rural locations say they feel stressed on a daily basis. Other popular 'stress busters' were a walk in the park (33 per cent), hearing birdsong (14 per cent) and the smell of cut grass (10 per cent). Just imagine walking casually through a park in Sea View Road, hand in hand with your loved one, birds singing in the trees and the park-keeper mowing the grass … lovely!

A less obvious stress buster is shopping, or, to be more accurate, impulse buying and extravagant shopping by premenstrual women. Professor Karen Pine of the University of Hertfordshire presented her work to the British Psychological Society in 2009 after interviewing 443 women aged 18 to 50. Almost two-thirds of the women in the later stages of their menstrual cycle, known as the luteal phase, admitted they had bought something on impulse, and many felt remorseful. Most of the purchases were to do with adornment – jewellery, make-up and high heels – so perhaps it has something to do with dressing to impress during their fertile period. Further good news for men comes from Professor Pine: 'If women were worried about their shopping behaviour they might avoid going shopping in the week before their period is due.'

With so many stresses in our life, thank goodness for the wonderful NHS. The NHS was created in post-war Britain by the National Health Service Act 1946 (it does what it says on the tin), on 5 July 1948. According to the NHS's own website, the NHS was 'born out of a long-held ideal that good healthcare should be available to all, regardless of wealth'. At its heart were three core principles: that it should meet the needs of everyone, that it should be free at the point of delivery and that it should be based on clinical need, not ability to pay. These three principles have guided the development of the NHS over more than half a century and remain today. The government's budgets for 2008/09 show expenditure on the Health Service of £94 billion, which is quite a lot of money, so the good work goes on.

There are approximately 170,000 hospital beds in the UK with usage running at approximately 85 per cent. The NHS is increasingly finding itself under financial threat from litigation for negligence, in my opinion not really because the quality of care is decreasing but more owing to the fact that solicitors can now advertise 'no win/no fee' arrangements. In our USA-influenced litigious world, there is no such thing as an accident; it has to be someone's fault. Therefore, whoever's fault it is, they must be sued and this leaves no room for less than perfection.

Surely, negligence is very different from less than perfect? If we expect our health carers to be perfect we will often be disappointed. In 2008 the NHS set aside a record £787 million to cover the cost of claims and in 2009 it faced over 6,000 medical negligence cases. In 2008 solicitors suing the NHS received over £91 million pounds in costs, which was virtually three times the amount received by solicitors defending the NHS. That, in total, is £120 million in legal fees involving litigation and the NHS. On the bright side, at least the lawyers stay out of hospital by avoiding stress over their finances.

However, when you or your loved ones are really ill, NHS care is always there for you, instantly and at no cost, except strangely when it comes to parking your car in their car park. This is not the case in the United States as I remember to my cost (well, actually my insurance company's cost). I waited once in a walk-in hospital for care, with a temperature of 104°, and was asked to sign my credit card voucher as I slipped in and out of full consciousness. I duly managed to sign and I have to say the care was then magnificent. You could say Barclaycard saved my life.

If we are to continue with a free NHS then surely some financing changes are necessary. Rather than hit relatives and patients with car parking charges, insufficient-sized car parks and thus increased stress levels, which as we know in turn generates more ill health; how about charging patients for meals? One has to say that hospital food is invariably appalling, although I can appreciate that cooking for often thousands of people, sometimes three-quarters of a mile away from the kitchen, is challenging.

You do get what you pay for in life and it's worth remembering that every single person in a hospital pays for their own food when at home. If we all had to pay for our meals while in hospital, albeit at a subsidised rate, it would have an enormous effect upon NHS budgets and we could increase car park sizes, get rid of car park charges and importantly improve the quality of food. For instance, we could even have three grades of meals, A, B and C, with each costing different amounts per day. Why not? It parallels real life and you could even ensure Meal C's cost was no more than a couple of hours' car parking charge. I know such a scheme would be criticised but why should we pay nothing for food when in hospital?

None of us want to be ill, although if you had to design a system to ensure the maximum spread of infection, you more than likely would create a process whereby you would put all the really ill people together in a small room with no natural ventilation, closely seated together, sharing their viruses by all means possible – coughing, sneezing, hands on chairs and shared toilet facilities. This should work well and then we could call these places doctor's waiting rooms.

Hospitals can also be dangerous places; they are full of people who are ill, so the sooner one gets out, the better. If you need an operation the modern trend is to get you out afterwards as soon as possible. If one has to have an operation, hopefully the anaesthetic works properly but if one does find oneself horribly half-awake on the operating table there are certain things you do not want to hear the consultant surgeon saying: 'What's he in for again?' or 'Hang on, if that's his kidney, what's this?' or the disconcerting 'Wasn't that an incredible stag night last night?', the frightening 'Isn't that the guy who ran off with your wife?' or the worrying 'Has someone been using these knives to eat their lunch again?' Perhaps worst of all would be: 'Big day today, first one back after my suspension.'

Too much of anything is obviously bad for you, and will more than likely adversely affect your health. Unfortunately, excess is a common human condition, which brings us suitably to the next subject: human vice.

19

Caught in a Vice

Life is full of temptations, most of which are bad for our health, but isn't that the great attraction of a vice, that it's naughty? Just like Luke Skywalker in *Star Wars*, we continuously have two forces pulling at us: the light side and the Darth Vader side and sometimes the dark side wins! Unfortunately for society, in the case of a very small minority of our citizens, the dark side *regularly* wins.

In a civilised society we need rules and regulations and consequences for overstepping the mark; otherwise daily life would be chaotic and anarchic. Thus we have created laws to regulate society's operation in an attempt to dissuade people from going to the dark side. Our politicians make these laws and, as we live in a democracy and if we don't like these laws, of course we can vote the politicians out, or at least that's the theory.

People have erred off the law-abiding track since time immemorial and as a result we have been given guidance on human sins for centuries. Pope Gregory the Great listed the original Seven Deadly Sins as follows: *superbia* (pride), *invidia* (envy), *ira* (anger), *avaritia* (avarice), *tristia* (sadness), *guls* (gluttony) and *luxuria* (lust). Sadness was subsequently replaced by sloth, which if you can be bothered to be interested in this change, was a sad occasion indeed.

In the manner of so many things nowadays these Seven Deadly Sins were re-engineered for modern consumption by the Vatican in 2008, when the new deadly sins became: environmental pollution, genetic manipulation, accumulating excessive wealth, inflicting poverty, drug trafficking and consumption, morally debateable experiments and violations of the fundamental rights of human nature. Heaven help you, if by chance you are a wealthy Californian genetic scientist who smokes the odd bit of grass and doesn't recycle your cornflake boxes – hell beckons!

These new sins appear far less personal and more aligned to society's vices rather than an individual's misdemeanours. Somehow I just can't imagine Sicilians flocking to church and confessing to not having recycled their cardboard pizza boxes. Presumably, the upside is that it is now OK to be proud, envious, gluttonous, lustful, angry, greedy and lazy and, if so, thank goodness for that! Here are some ideas on a number of even more modern Seven Deadly Sins: knife crime, binge drinking, wearing hoodies, carjacking and, of course, producing reality TV shows.

In the UK the Criminal Justice System (CJS) covers the agencies of police, the Crown Prosecution Service, the courts and the National Offender Management Service, all working together to deliver our nation's criminal justice. The work of these agencies is overseen by three government departments: the Ministry of Justice, the Home Office and the Attorney General's Office. According to the Criminal Justice Service's own website these departments and agencies 'are working together to reform and improve the Criminal Justice System'. Interestingly, they use the word 'reform', which I take to imply it needs changing for the better, like a jailed prisoner.

The stated purpose of the CJS is grand, praiseworthy and practically unchallengeable: 'To deliver justice for all, by convicting and punishing the guilty and helping them to stop offending, while protecting the innocent.' Bravo! The problem is they just don't have enough resources to do this to the satisfaction of their customers who, of course, are you and me.

In 1981 there were approximately 11 million crimes reported to the British Crime Survey and in 2007/08 this figure was 10 million; so much for the commonly held view that we live in a dramatically more dangerous society than in times past. This figure peaked in 1995 at 19.4 million reported crimes, although I have to say I don't recall the mid-1990s being particularly lawless. I do remember wanting to pummel a few yuppies, but that's all.

The number of crimes recorded by police in 2007/08 was only 5.4 million, which means that approximately half of all crimes are not reported to police, which is worrying. The key reoffending rate was 58 per cent of prisoners leaving prison and reoffending within two years, or more accurately *caught* reoffending within two years! Denmark's reoffending rate is approximately 45 per cent and

Australia is reported at 38 per cent (so yet another win for the Aussies). It seems those convicts have finally reformed.

In 2007/08 theft and handling stolen goods represented one-third of all crimes while crimes involving firearms in England and Wales totalled 17,300. In the 1980s we had a prison population of approximately 45,000 whereas today we have nearly double this figure. Twice the number of people in jail and 10 per cent less crimes, and yet public perception is that sentences are insufficient and weak. How is this the case?

In fact, over two-thirds of men sent to prison receive sentences of one year or less. However, crime isn't just a British problem: 8.75 million people are estimated to be incarcerated worldwide at any one time. Take a moment to consider the magnitude of this number. We lock away nearly 9 million of our fellow citizens who live with us in our home, planet Earth.

In the league table of prisoners per capita the USA is a clear first, with 686 citizens per 100,000 of population in jail, which is almost one in every 145 of the US population (the equivalent of two jail-birds in the little road in which I grew up). Quite amazingly that little tropical paradise of the Cayman Islands comes second at 664. It must be the heat that gets to them! Our much-loved Kazakhstan is fifth with 552 prisoners per 100,000, and I notice an intriguing link here between not signing global warming treaties and criminal activities – another statistic for Al Gore to use. In the UK we are only running at 139 prisoners per 100,000 which is approximately one-fifth of the US rate, although needless to say the Australians beat us again at 110 per 100,000.

One statistic that is not given enough analysis is the amount of crime carried out by women. Women constitute only about 6 per cent of the UK's prison population, although they represent 50.5 per cent of the population. Therefore, using simple arithmetic, it seems that men are 16 times more likely to get caught for a crime than a woman. Are women craftier or are they 16 times more honest? I merely ask the question.

In the UK, not unsurprisingly 90 per cent of all murders are committed by males and, if my wife does commit the perfect crime and murder me, at least she would be in a minority! In 2008/09 there were 648 murders in England and Wales, and for the loved ones of these victims their sentence of emotional trauma at the loss of their dear family member is for life. I'm sure this statistic would not match public perception, quite simply because of the high-profile media coverage of horrendous murders. If you asked a range of British citizens to guess the number of murders each year in our country, they would probably come up with a number in the thousands and perhaps even tens of thousands. An answer of 600 odd would be highly unlikely and so when they tell you at the end of *Crimewatch*, 'Don't worry', you can believe them, as they are not *conning* you.

Colombia has the highest murder rate per capita, closely followed by South Africa. For most sane people it is unimaginable how a fellow human being could take the life of another person, as surely above all else, life is sacred. English law defines murder as 'the unlawful killing of a human being, under the Queen's Peace with malice aforethought'. The victim no longer has to be a reasonable creature nor has to die within a year and a day of the offence, both archaic and crazy stipulations.

Because the USA has so many murders they seem to have to break them down into three degrees: First Degree Murder, which is intentional killing; Second Degree Murder, which is homicide committed as a principal or accomplice in the perpetration of a felony; and Third Degree Murder, which is any other murder when the intent was not to kill but to harm the victim.

The conundrum for any government is plain to see: people *learn* how to become better criminals while in prison. It currently costs approximately £37,500 a year to keep an individual in prison. Therefore, surely for both these reasons we want as few people as possible in prison, which is exactly the opposite of what popular culture is demanding. However, on the flipside, society wants to feel justice is done. If a crime is committed, it wants to know, first, that it is more than likely it will be solved; second, that there will be a fair sentence; and third, that the criminal is unlikely to reoffend. This is all perfectly reasonable but in danger of becoming a mirage for modern society.

The government estimates that half of all crimes in the UK are committed by fewer than 100,000 people. Locking them up clearly isn't the sole answer, as the USA has both the highest prison population per capita and one of the highest murder rates. It truly is a conundrum for a civilised society, but at all costs let's ensure that the dark side doesn't win.

It's all a far cry from policing in the 1950s and 1960s when people deeply respected the police and were somewhat in awe of their power and understood the police's place in society. Stealing some apples from a local orchard (scrumping) was the extent of crime in my small Hampshire town back in the 1960s. Surely policing is all about *Dixon of Dock Green*, *Z Cars*, *Juliet Bravo* or the more modern version of this nostalgic viewpoint, *Heartbeat*? However, despite this rose-tinted perspective on the past, one has to admit that during this era there were the Moors Murderers, gangsters ruled the East End of London, and fighting outside pubs on a Saturday night was also fairly prevalent, even then.

I suspect the biggest change is in respect of theft and petty crime (you really could leave your doors unlocked then). Most experts agree that the underlying causes for the increase in these types of crimes are drink and drugs. These truly are the bane of modern society and particularly British society. Addiction is a serious problem and, according to Smart Justice, 30 per cent of the female prisoners in the UK are in jail due to drug offences. According to the 2004/2005 British Crime Survey, 18 per cent of victims believed their attacker was under the influence of alcohol and 29 per cent of robbery victims believed the thief to be under the influence of drugs. Reconviction is driven by the need for cash to buy drugs. Class A drugs are estimated to cost an addict around £600 a week while a crack cocaine addict might need up to an incredible £1,100 a week to feed their habit, and this is after tax.

The real problem is confirmed from the horse's mouth because 63 per cent of male prisoners in 2003 admitted to hazardous drinking prior to their offence and 47 per cent of all victims of violence described their assailant as being under the influence of alcohol. It seems that to reduce crime we need to reduce addiction, which is simple to say but difficult to achieve. What would Obi-Wan Kinobi do about all this? Turn to the Force, of course.

Before we get too depressed with all this talk of crime and law-breaking it's worth remembering that not all criminals are very good at their chosen career path; in fact many criminals are bad at what they do. South African police claim to have arrested the dumbest criminal in Pretoria. The man walked into a police station and reported that he had been held up at gunpoint by a terrifying gang who stole his mobile phone. The concerned detective then phoned the stolen mobile phone number, only to find it ringing in the complainant's pocket! Not unsurprisingly he was then arrested for perjury. What a heist!

However, we have our own incompetent thieves of which we, too, can be 'proud'. Burglar John Pearce made a less than perfect getaway after breaking into a house in Kent. He was found hanging upside down from a window with his foot stuck, no doubt peering head-first into some prickly bushes. Andrew Kellet was given an ASBO banning him from boasting of his high-speed car chases, thefts, drug taking and, worst of all, criminal damage to a wheelie bin, after he posted his criminal antics on YouTube. Please note, he was also banned from performing these criminal acts! He asserts that he was 'not Britain's dumbest criminal. I'm just misunderstood'. He could have a point, you know, but only because there are others who are even less skilled in their dastardly pursuits. Peter Addison, for example, actually wrote on the wall of his crime scene: 'Peter Addison was here.' This helpfully enabled the police to hunt him down and then identify him. They even found him wearing a T-shirt stolen from the crime scene. Even Agatha Christie couldn't make this mystery last long!

Thieves the world over have lost their way in life and none more so than a Vancouver criminal who robbed a gas station at knifepoint to be chased at high speed by the Canadian cops. He should have known the Mounties always get their man, although the police were helped enormously by the thief getting lost during the chase and pulling into a gas station to ask directions and, you guessed it, at the very same gas station he had robbed earlier.

Even the police can get lost though and with this in mind the Metropolitan Police introduced a trial microchip system to keep track of officers using the new Automated Personal Location System (APLS). Of course its intention is to aid communication and effective direction of officers, but you can guarantee that some 'Helen' at HQ will let them know when they have 'left the designated road system' (see Chapter 13).

We have always had a strange morbid fascination with crime and the police, which is reflected by an array of films on the subject and a regular dose of police-based TV programmes, from the inevitable reality shows to long-running dramas such as *The Bill*, *Midsomer Murders*, *A Touch of Frost*, *Silent Witness* and *Waking the Dead*. Even comedy needs crime: think of *The Lavender Hill Mob*, *The Pink Panther* or *Stir Crazy*. Most of the time the cops win and we can all feel the right level of relief, reassurance and, of course, the necessary retribution: 'Go on punk, make my day!'

Perhaps our fascination with crime is driven by a subconscious feeling that 'There but for the grace of God go I.' Interestingly this phrase emanates from John Bradford (1510 to 1555) – an English Reformer and martyr who, while imprisoned in the Tower of London, uttered these words, or something like them, when he saw a criminal going to execution.

Before you get too indignant about all this, it's worth considering some research by Susanne Kartedt and Stephen Farrall. According to the BBC these two academics surveyed 1,807 adults in England and Wales and found that a staggering 61 per cent admitted to having committed a crime at some point. Before you completely give up on the human race let's review some of the crimes: paying in cash for a building job, taking something from work (as small as a paper clip) or exaggerating insurance claims – none of which I condone, of course.

Apparently, the latest crime to add to this list is that of 'having a birthday BBQ'. The BBC reported a daring police raid involving a helicopter, four police cars and a riot van on Andrew Poole's thirtieth birthday BBQ in Sowton near Exeter in July 2009. Locals feared a rave after spotting a posting on the Internet and informed the police, although as Andrew said, 'What effectively the police did was come in and stop 15 people eating burgers.' The event was closed down under Section 63 of the Criminal Justice and Public Order Act 1994, and we can all again sleep in peace.

Further evidence of the reassurance our police force can provide us with was the excellent advice given by the Avon and Somerset Constabulary to deter thieves and burglars. Their suggestion to homeowners is to use defensive planting of prickly bushes around drainpipes or beneath ground-floor windows to enhance home security. The only problem that might arise is if the criminal fraternity discover the existence of pruning secateurs.

If only we could go back in time and enjoy again the era when this type of advice was unnecessary. However, perhaps we can, as Huddersfield police are re-energising an old police box in Almondbury as a base for the village's community-support officers. Sergeant John MacFadzean from the West Yorkshire Police said, 'It's going back to traditional values. I think they see the box as going back to the good old days.' Doctor Who, please take us back in your Tardis to a more peaceful time.

Still at least when a criminal does get to court we can rely upon the jury system. Around 400,000 people are summoned each year to appear as jurors and of course this is a legal obligation, not a polite request. You do not get paid for jury service, although you can claim allowable financial loss, reasonable travel expenses and a daily allowance towards refreshments. Please be warned, this expense claim form is not like your semi-fictional office claim, so be accurate with your entries … or else!

I found my own jury service quite inspiring, fascinating and rewarding, and I gather this isn't unusual. I was particularly impressed by my co-jurors. We were all from different walks of life, with varying ages, experience, communication skills, attitudes and beliefs, as indeed we needed to be. However, every single man and woman in the jury deeply respected the magnitude of their responsibilities especially when we retired to decide upon our verdict. I was hugely impressed by the way we all went about this task and I left my jury service with an enhanced respect for both society's majority and the jury system. The lunches weren't bad either!

Heaven help those people who are called to jury service on a serial killer's trial. Thankfully these psychopathic killers are rare, with fewer than 400 known serial killers in recorded history. A serial killer is generally defined as an individual who murders three or more people, in three or more separate events over a period of time and for their own warped psychological reasons. Obviously the data on serial killers is patchy and some appear to have got away with their crimes completely. Reassuringly, most do get caught – Jack the Ripper is an exception to the rule.

I hope our apparent fascination with serial killers arises more out of a fear of such illogical, cruel and calculated evil acts, rather than a desire to engage with such evil. However, our fascination is confirmed by our need to give each of these vile human beings a nickname. Normally we give nicknames only to close buddies or much-loved pets – not to scary mass murderers! Consider this list: the Green River Killer – Gary Ridgway, USA, 48 known murders; the Chessboard Killer – Alexander Pichushkin, Russia, 48 known murders; the Angel of Death – Donald Harvey, USA, 37 known murders; the Killer Clown – John Wayne Gacy, USA, 33 known murders; the Yorkshire Ripper – Peter Sutcliffe, UK 13 known murders; and the Moors Murderers – Ian Brady and Myra Hindley, UK, 5 known murders. There are plenty more from all around the world: the Candyman, the Tehran Desert Vampire, the Railroad Killer, the BTK Killer, the Vampire of Düsseldorf, the Baton Rouge Killer, Son of Sam, the Granny Killer and the Brooklyn Strangler. Every nickname is so menacing and their crimes are so terrifying, so why do we give each of them catchy titles? It's very perplexing.

Unfortunately, in the UK we hold the unwanted record of the highest number of killings by a serial killer: Dr Harold Shipman was found guilty of a horrendous 218 confirmed killings. The vast majority of serial killers are men and the country where most occur, or at least are recorded, is the USA, with approximately 120 serial killers. Very disturbingly, in the UK we come a clear second with 42 and equal third, each on 14, are Germany, France and Australia. Do you notice a trend here, of so-called highly evolved Western cultures breeding murderous psychopathic crazies?

The good news is that most of these evil acts are punished by life sentences or execution, although one notable exception was Pedro Alonso Lopez, the Beast of the Andes, who killed 71 known innocent people and allegedly up to 300, but was deported and released from jail in Ecuador to Columbia, 'for good behaviour'!

The modern media are very quick to enlighten us the minute that incidents occur and quickly jump on the bandwagon of any news story such as knife crimes. This encourages the public to lose some perspective and worry, often excessively, about the dangers. Because being the victim of crime is a horrible thing and quite understandably we have some fears about this, it is possible to lose some perspective. The reality is that you most likely can sleep in peace in your bed tonight. The vast majority of us are decent hard-working, tax-paying and honest people, and isn't that just heart-warming? You just have to watch out for those obvious exceptions – the people who get caught on CCTV and appear on *Crimewatch*.

You can rest assured that, with the exception of stealing paper clips from work, your neighbours are more than likely there to support you, not steal from you, so sleep tight tonight, which brings us suitably to the next subject: sleep.

20

Sleep Tight, My Love

The one place in our life where we need to feel safe and secure is in our own bed. This is our haven from the rigours of life and a place where we can escape to peace and tranquillity, at least in theory. Unfortunately, many of us take our troubles and strife to bed with us; not one's spouse, but one's stresses in life. Well, on second thoughts maybe it is one's spouse!

However, the reality is that these troubles do affect our sleep patterns and stress is often the most likely cause of sleep dysfunction. We need our sleep because without it we cannot function effectively and, contrary to conventional wisdom, it is not the need to re-energise that sleep meets, it is the need for brain development. A significant 18 per cent of British people survive on less than six hours sleep a night. The record for the longest period without sleep is held by Randy Gardner (not an aroused horticulturalist, but a 17-year-old high school student) who stayed awake for 264 continuous hours. Four days into this marathon Randy didn't feel in the slightest bit like his name, but had started hallucinating and believed he was a famous sportsman. Silly boy!

Sleep doesn't really save energy either, because during eight hours of sleep we only save approximately 50 calories, which is less than contained in a Sainsbury's strawberry fat-free yogurt. Lack of sleep produces lethargy, irritability, forgetfulness and attention deficit, and scientists estimate that after 17 hours of wakefulness, for instance waking up at 8 a.m. and not going to bed until 1 a.m., there is a decrease in attention to the same level as drinking alcohol equivalent to the legal drink driving limit. You can see a time in the future where police stop you while you were driving late at night and do a 'yawn-alyser' on you just to check you are fit to drive!

According to the 2006 US Bureau of Labour Statistics the average sleep hours per day is highest for men at 9.7 hours when they are aged 15 to 19, and lowest at 8.2 hours when they are aged 45 to 54. This then rises again to reach 9.0 hours a day for those aged over 65 years. However, an average figure hides extremes and of course Margaret Thatcher famously functioned with less than four hours' sleep a night. Whether you liked Maggie's style of leadership or not, you could never call her a snake, because pythons need 18 hours of sleep a day.

There are real dangers in sleep dysfunction and the US National Association of Home Builders has predicted that by the year 2015 nearly 60 per cent of custom-built homes will have two master bedrooms to enable couples to sleep apart. The reasons for this are considered to be snoring, night-time toilet breaks, shift working, childcare and insomnia. I can't help feeling this is a backward step and this trend cannot have a positive impact upon couples' romantic interactions or relationships generally. Perhaps houses of the future will have both a husband's master bedroom and a wife's master bedroom with a bathroom in between, plus a boudoir for night-time liaisons, set up with candles, soft music and warm lighting. I hope not.

The influential think-tank Demos reported that a century ago we slept on average 9 hours a night, but now across all age groups and genders it's down to 7.75 hours a night, which is approximately 15 per cent less – the stresses of modern life are without doubt the reason. It's getting so desperate that workers in the USA can now get a nice power nap at a specially designed facility run by MetroNap in New York – $14 for a 20-minute nap.

Business people now regularly travel across the Atlantic and for those who have regularly flown this route you will know only too well the strains on the body caused by jet lag. Dr Kwangwook Cho of the University of Bristol conducted a small study of women aged between 22 and 28 who had worked for at least five years for an airline. Jet lag occurs when a person crosses a number of time zones, disrupting the body's circadian rhythms. Dr Cho found aircrew that had a shorter period of turn-around had an area of the brain called the temporal lobe that was noticeably smaller than people who hadn't suffered jet lag. In my own experience I find I need several days to recover from a transatlantic flight and it gets harder as you get older, like most things – though with one notable exception!

However, there is hope if you fly to Australia, because Swiss researchers have found that playing the didgeridoo for 25 minutes a day helps with sleep apnoea. The team from the Zuercher Hoehenklinik Wald hospital found that training the upper airways by using didgeridoos improved sleep-related outcomes. This all makes perfect sense really because Rolf Harris is obviously a deeply relaxed kind of man and now we know why – he always gets a good night's sleep! As Rolf would say, 'Tie me kangaroo down, sport. Sample me wombat black, Jack. Keep me cockatoo cool, Curl. Take me koala back, Jack. Mind me platypus duck, Bill. Tie me kangaroo down ...' What sort of nightmare was that, Rolf?

One sleeping danger that always arouses passions is that of snoring and this is because a partner's snoring is a major irritation, particularly for light-sleeping ladies, and as for the snorer, they feel unreasonably attacked for something beyond their control. It's a recipe for friction and that's the problem because collapsed airways cause vibration and friction, and thus noise.

The 1992 British snoring champion Melvin Switzer blasted out 92 decibels, which is very loud indeed, and unfortunately, or perhaps even fortunately, his wife Julie was deaf in one ear. However, their neighbours weren't so understanding as Melvin reported that eight neighbours had moved away in a ten-year period. The average snore volume is 40 to 69 decibels. It is estimated by the BSSAA that about 15 million British people snore, of which about two-thirds are men. For those of us who snore, we share this 'hobby' with illustrious previous fellow snorers such as George Washington and Winston Churchill.

A study commissioned by the hotel chain Travelodge found that Coventry was the UK's loudest snore-spot and they identified five distinct types of snorer (and snore): the Snorter – a horse-like snort; the Snorchestra – long low snores that build to a crescendo; the McEnroe – violent grunting ('Never, you cannot be serious!');

the Walrus – continuous groaning; and the Old Banger – noises like a spluttering engine. My wife tells me I'm a Snorchestra. What she doesn't know is that she is a gentle Old Banger herself. Relate, here we come.

However, it's not all bad news, as a team from the University of California San Francisco has found that heavy snorers burned an extra 373 calories a day which equates to a vigorous 30-minute gym workout. Therefore, my snoring may reduce my chances of survival if downed in the English Channel, but it does form part of my new weight-loss programme.

Experts give advice upon ways to reduce one's snoring: avoiding alcohol, losing weight (by snoring of course), sleeping on your side, using a humidifier, avoiding eating late or taking sleeping tablets. Unfortunately, consumer watchdog *Which?* found that in many cases most over-the-counter remedies just didn't work and in fact 71 per cent of people surveyed found that seven selected aids were 'not very effective' or 'not effective at all'. They should have asked the snorers not their spouses.

However, I think I have found a scapegoat for my snoring and that is my early childhood pet dog, Kim. Not only did we unfairly blame her for the unpleasant smells in the lounge after a heavy family meal but now it seems she might be to blame for my snoring. The University Hospital Umea spoke to 15,556 people regarding snoring and found that being exposed to a dog as a newborn boosted the risk of snoring by 26 per cent. Bad dog!

This may not be a laughing matter as the US Army found that just a couple of sleepless nights can impact upon our moral judgement. Dr William Killgore of the Walter Reed Army Institute of Research said, 'Our results simply suggest that when sleep deprived, individuals appear to be selectively slower in deliberations about moral dilemmas.' Perhaps the real answer to the question 'Why did Darth Vader go over to the dark side?' is simply 'Because his wife snored.'

We all need to sleep well and particularly to get into Repetitive

Eye Movement (REM) mode, as it is during this state that our brains get the nurturing they need and then we can again be Shiny Happy People. In REM mode we can have the deep dreams that are necessary to maintain our sanity, exfoliate our fears and imagine all manner of creative potential, including being a member of a famous American Indie rock band.

Apparently, we have at least four or five dreams in a normal night's sleep and if someone says they don't dream, this simply means they cannot remember their dreams. A lifetime's dreaming equates to about six solid years, so what manner of bizarre imaginings do we conjure up in these six years? Thank goodness we can't remember most of them. Mary Shelley claimed the idea for *Frankenstein* came to her in a dream, so beware.

Do you ever wake up in mid-dream, possibly to visit the bathroom, and want to quickly get back to sleep to return to your dream's fantasy world? Seemingly you cannot dream while snoring, and alcohol and prescription drugs can cause nightmares. Studies have shown that woman dream equally of men and women, whereas men dream more of other men. This is surprising, isn't it? Nearly two-thirds of us have recurring dreams and close to half of us say we dream of things that subsequently came true. This is very worrying, because if there is even a 42-per-cent chance that my dream last night about Paris Hilton, dominoes, marquetry, pet dogs, Luke Skywalker and my satnav, Helen, is going to come true, I'm going to need some intensive therapy!

A study by researchers at the University of California San Diego has concluded that problems are more likely to be solved after a period of dreamy sleep. The Beatles' song 'Yesterday', one of the world's most-covered pieces of music, was apparently created from a melody that appeared in a Paul McCartney dream, and many other creative people refer to their dream as the breakthrough in a piece of work. Most of the dreams I recall don't involve a creative inspiration, breathtaking vision or insight into life's mysteries. They tend to involve my deepest fears that are nicely dropped by my subconscious mind into a weird and bizarre sleep-world involving a myriad of characters, who in real life would never find themselves together in one room.

The classic dreams apparently involve: being chased (with your feet feeling like lead), being lost (where no one knows you), falling (strangely with no ground to hit), flying ('I'm flying through the air' – Snowman), becoming separated from a loved one (not the divorce type), public nudity (why is it always me that's naked, not Kate Winslet), drowning (not in debt), your phone not working (the modern number one fear) and, of course, the infidelity of your sexual partner. I love the way we are angry at our partner when we wake up because they were, in our fear-based dream, living out our deepest worries. How dare they! Do you find that eventually you end up apologising for being in their dream and doing what they imagined? Still, it keeps the peace.

One fascinating condition that a few people suffer from is somnambulism or sleepwalking. A Finnish study in 1997 found that approximately 6 per cent of children sleepwalked and the figure for adults was around 3.5 per cent. One of the most famous sleep-walkers was Donald Duck in the 1947 Disney film *Sleepy Time* – 'Oh boy, oh boy, oh boy!' Sleepwalkers can be a danger to themselves but some of their non-fatal nocturnal pursuits include: urinating in cupboards (yuck), talking (usually gibberish), dressing (a great excuse for trying on the wife's dress), painting (not the Mona Lisa but your neighbour's beloved BMW with white emulsion), dancing (Abba style), and, believe it or not, sexual intercourse!

NREM Arousal Parasomnia (sexsomnia) is a new form of sleep disorder or at least a newly discovered form of dysfunction. The first research paper on the subject was published in 1996 at the University of Toronto and in 2005 the whole issue came to a head in the UK when the *Sun* reported the story from Canada where a man was acquitted of sexual assault, with sexsomnia as his main defence. Other cases followed in the UK, Australia and the USA.

What a frustration for the sufferers, though, as they can't even remember it happening. You can imagine a new *Sun* headline on the subject of sexsomnia: 'Sex sleep keeps you up at night.' When researching the subject of 'sleep sex' on the Internet, I inadvertently typed into the search box an *h* instead of an *l* and, believe me, this was an extremely unsettling experience!

As far as I can see one sure solution to this disorder is to sleep with four layers of clothes on your body, because by the time you would have unbuckled two belts, taken off several layers of T-shirts, shoes and socks, you would be bound to have woken up.

An ABS News poll called the American Sex Survey found that 31 per cent of men and 14 per cent of women regularly sleep in the nude. The hotel chain Travelodge reported that they are now leaving towels in reception to cover up guests who sleepwalk naked to maintain some modesty, although the miniscule size and roughness of many hotel towels (not Travelodge's, of course) could easily cause even further embarrassment to a sleepwalking guest.

One solution to stop a sexsomniac in their tracks is, according to Italian researchers, to have a TV in the bedroom. The Italian psychologist and sexologist Serenella Salomoni quizzed 523 Italian couples and found that those without a TV in the bedroom had sex twice as much as couples with a TV in their bedroom. If this isn't bad enough, for the over-50s the average goes from seven times a month without a TV in the bedroom, to 1.5 times a month with a TV in the bedroom – and I'm not talking about episodes of *EastEnders*. Incidentally, what does point five of sex feel like, or is this a new type of Vatican-approved Italian birth-control technique?

The survey found that what a couple watched on the television had a marked effect upon the couple's mood and appetite for love. Violent films put half of the couples completely off sensual activity and reality TV left a third of couples frigid (don't forget the *f*). US researchers at the University of Pennsylvania found that almost half of Americans had 'TV watching' as their prominent pre-sleep activity. A study at Colombia University and a health-care institute in New York found that 40 per cent of children had a TV in their bedroom and that those with a TV in their bedroom were more likely to be overweight – TV dinners and midnight snacking rules!

Teenagers are renowned for their laziness and prevalence to sleep in late. Professor Russell Foster at Brasenose College, Oxford may offer a different perspective when he said of people aged 10 to 20, 'There's a biological predisposition for going to bed late and getting up late.' It really is hormonal then.

A study by Columbia University Medical Center found that teenagers who went to sleep after midnight were 25 per cent more likely to suffer from depression and 20 per cent more likely to have suicidal thoughts. However, there may be other reasons why teenagers don't get a good night's sleep. A study by researchers at Sahlgren's Academy in Gothenburg found that teenagers who used their mobile phones a lot were more prone to disrupted sleep, restlessness, stress and fatigue. Of course, there is just the chance that it is the teenagers who can't sleep who fill their time by phoning or texting friends.

A comfortable bed is a truly wonderful thing and there is no bed as comfortable as your own. It is a haven from life's stresses and a place to recharge the brain's batteries. Unfortunately, as you get older the good old bladder seems to lose some degree of traction and from the age of about 40, at around 5 a.m. you are woken by the need to visit the bathroom and that strange bedclothes lifting thing that happens to male bodies when you are ready for nuptial toilet action!

When you return to bed those last extra two hours of sleep are blissful, aren't they? However, if you have some worries it's exactly when you get back into bed at 5.05 a.m. that your subconscious mind turns on the thought traffic jams. Once this happens you may as well get up and watch the QVC or one of those workout programmes from a beach in California.

Our subconscious minds are powerful things and one of the best ways to understand the subconscious mind is to consider a couple of imaginary situations. If you were faced with a wooden plank, two feet wide, placed across a ravine with a 1,000-feet drop, you would more than likely say, 'No way I'm crossing that! I'm staying where I am. That looks dangerous.' Your conscious and subconscious minds would be working in perfect harmony and looking after you. This is despite the fact that if the same plank was placed on your lounge floor you would willingly walk across it, but 1,000 feet up, no! However, if a hungry lion ran at you, there is little doubt you would instantly scamper straight across the ravine. In a millisecond your subconscious mind would assess the risks and come to the conclusion that the lion was the greater risk. This is impressive.

While we sleep our subconscious mind keeps us breathing and listens out for strange noises. It is this very same subconscious mind that wakes us exactly one minute before the alarm clock is due to go off. The fear of burglary is a real and unpleasant fear for many of us and our home truly is our castle, and perhaps this is another reason to avoid sleeping naked. Bad enough to have to confront a burglar, but in the nude, oh no!

Sleeping away from your own bed is never as relaxing as sleeping in your own bed. I find hotel bedrooms slightly unsettling and never sleep as I do at home. It's probably the banging doors at 5.22 a.m. when your sales representative neighbour leaves his room to get on to the road early, or the ridiculously over-warm rooms, or the noisy air conditioning, or sometimes, if you are particularly unlucky, the previous guest's 6.02 a.m. wake-up call.

Wherever we lay our heads, a long, deep, peaceful night of sleep is one of the great joys in life. Personally I love sleeping and never see it as wasted 'Thatcher-style' time, but rather as theme-park time for my subconscious mind. Tonight I have decided to think of Kate Winslet just before I close my eyes and see what happens as my subconscious mind runs riot probably creating a scene of Michael Fish and Goofy playing dominoes together in the middle of a bowling alley.

Whatever forms our dreams take, you can guarantee they usually involve off-the-wall experiences and don't feature a simple happy time, which brings us suitably to the next subject: happiness.

21

Happy Smiley People

Everyone wants to be happy and a good night's sleep sets the day off exactly how you would want it to start: fresh, relaxed, ready for fun, new experiences and a stack of fulfilment ... well, that's the plan at least. For thousands of years mankind has chased the ultimate goal of happiness and generation after generation of us have been in pursuit of this, often oasis-style, mirage. Because of this you would have thought that by now we would have worked out the true nature of happiness.

Before we explore the science of happiness let's just consider the simple value of smiling and laughing. We all know laughing is contagious and the late Tommy Cooper's act relied upon us joining in with him laughing at himself. Smiling really is quite simple because you only need five pairs of facial muscles to smile, but if you are really in the mood for some frivolity you can expand a smile into up to 53 muscles. There are 18 types of smile and scientists have confirmed we can instinctively tell the difference between a faked social smile and a heartfelt Duchenne smile. Interestingly, even a faked smile gives us a warm feeling and of course smiling and laughing release those great endorphins, which like their fishy, similar-sounding friends, help us jump through hoops, squeak with delight and do a leap for joy.

Laughter is contagious and there is nothing much better than laughing out loud in an audience of other raucous laughers. Its great fun, isn't it? As an experiment why not try smiling at every person you come into contact with during a day? It's an amazing experience, as most people smile back at you. Before we get too carried away with this Pollyanna style of living, as with all things in life it's the minority that ruin it for the rest of us; because sooner or later you will smile at an angry man or woman and you will get the inevitable confrontational response, 'What's wrong with you? What's your problem?' I'm afraid this is the reason you can only keep it up for one day.

Not everyone is so fond of laughter and a primary school in Breightmet near Bolton recently fell foul of this when local residents signed a petition demanding action by Bolton Council against the 'unbearable screams of laughter' from the playground. The council subsequently found the laughter did not break the World Health Organisation limits, not on laughing, but on nuisance. The Japanese are clearly more in the mood for fun than the residents of Bolton because on 15 Tokyo railway stations, railway staff are being checked by computerised scanners to ensure they smile enough at customers; which is great for customer service but unfortunately it means *sayounara* to privacy.

Scientists have studied the theory of happiness for many years now and it is called the neuroscience of happiness, implying that happiness is created in the brain. In the 1950s James Olds and Peter Milner of McGill University in Canada studied the behaviour of rats that had had electrodes injected into their brains and as a result could be encouraged to perform certain acts and then be rewarded with an electric shot to just the right spot in their brains. Pleasure is measured or driven by our orbitofrontal cortex and some psychologists have created a formula for happiness which is: pleasure plus engagement, plus meaning, equals happiness. Engagement means being focused upon your life's activities and meaning involves having a clear purpose in your life, whether this is spiritual or otherwise. Unfortunately, we all need balance in our lives, because workaholics seem to have too much engagement and addicts have too much focus on one meaning, getting their fix.

I wonder whether scientists are the best people to be working on this important research, as surely happiness is primarily an emotion, not a logical thought and most of the scientists I have met abound with logic but are, let's just say, not naturally soft and cuddly. Aldous Huxley in his novel *Brave New World*, written in the 1930s, warned us about scientific control of such areas and when Robert Heath and his colleagues of Tublane University, New Orleans in the 1960s controversially experimented upon curing men of 'gayness', we perhaps should have known it had gone too far.

Pollsters GfK NOP surveyed 1,001 people in the UK and asked

237

what happiness meant to them. Very importantly the respondents, unlike in normal surveys where there is a prescribed list of answers to choose from, were able to choose their own answers. According to these 1,001 people, happiness can be summarised to derive from six key elements and these were: relationships, contentment, security, health, transcendence and fulfilment.

The strongest answer by far was relationships where 73 per cent of people included this as a key component of happiness, and why not? We all want to be loved and have someone to love. Contentment comes from being at peace with one's life and knowing where you are in your life and more importantly who you are. In our modern world, security is gained, not by a warm and dry cave away from prowling lions, but by money and all it offers. Health comes from feeling physically well and being able to do most of what you want. Transcendence is about feeling and seeing the bigger picture, something often underpinned by spiritual beliefs. Fulfilment comes from feeling engaged with one's life and the rewards that this engagement brings. All this sounds oh-so-easy, doesn't it? However, that's where the theory falls down and then life takes over.

Why don't we look at how life does intervene and why we need to remind ourselves that 'life's far too serious to take seriously'? Relationships – remember 36 per cent of men cite 'lack of sex' as the reason for their divorce! Contentment – remember even in the get-away-from-the-rat-race country of France they come 20th in the world suicide league table! Security – remember that according to the newspapers, 'we are in the worst financial crisis for 60 years'. Health – remember Christmas Day is the day when the most heart attacks occur! Transcendence – remember Bucks Fizz have reunited to undergo group cosmetic surgery. Fulfilment – remember that 11 out of 12 women still do the ironing.

Despite all this apparently overwhelming negative evidence, life really is all about perception and our personal perspective is our own reality of life. Is your glass half full or is it seven-eighths empty? To gain a more balanced perception of life let's revisit these six key happiness ingredients but with a different perspective. Relationships – we found that 73 per cent of people said their most valuable relationship was with their family. Contentment – we know there are plenty of opportunities in life for contentment, like a good marquetry session or being one of the 100,000 trainspotters in the UK. Security – in nuclear families 90 per cent of dads are the main breadwinners and successfully put a roof over their family's head. Health – average life expectancy in the UK has risen by 2,000 days over the last 25 years. Transcendence – 3 million people still go to church over Christmas. Fulfilment – if you win the lottery there is a 96-per-cent chance you won't feel worse!

Researchers at the British Household Panel Survey between 1991 and 2003 found that our happiness in life is 'smile-shaped', in other words in the shape of a 'U'. Based upon a happiness score of 'very happy' or 'fairly happy', we score high when we are in our early twenties with a 78 per cent happiness score. This gradually drops until we hit the lowest point in our mid-life-crisis forties, with a 70 per cent score and this reassuringly rises again from our fifties through to our seventies when we get to a peak happiness score of 80 per cent. The interesting factor is the low variance of 10 per cent between the high and low points in our lives and the confirmation that mid-life crisis does actually exist; although one could argue that a drop of 10 per cent is hardly a crisis.

However, before we get too smug, it is worth considering the results of a GfK NOP poll which found that our 'very happy' levels have fallen from a high in 1957 of 57 per cent to today's score, where only 36 per cent of people say they are 'very happy'. In the 1970s this figure was 34 per cent and in the late 1990s it was 30 per cent and it seems the Swinging Sixties made everybody very unsettled. These results are despite the fact that people today, compared to the 1950s, are more aware than ever of the importance of relationships, have more wealth, better health, greater leisure time, more interesting jobs and increased choice on virtually everything in life, except fresh vegetables straight from the garden. Happiness truly is an elusive, transitory and complex thing.

Needless to say, politicians are jumping on the happiness band-wagon because, if we are happy, we generally vote them in again and, if we are not happy, we throw them out. Conservative leader David Cameron said, 'We should be thinking not just what is good for putting money in people's pockets but what is good for putting joy in people's hearts.' Honourable aspirations, David, but let's just say the credit crunch hasn't helped much with this high-brow goal.

In 2002 the Prime Minister's strategic unit held a Life Satisfaction Seminar and later published an analytical paper which considered how happiness might affect different policies – of course they really meant our votes. According to the BBC Two series *The Happiness Formula*, the Department of Environment, Food and Rural Affairs was already working on a happiness index. Some eight years on from this strategic review, how do you feel they did with this aim of making us happy? Oops! Of course the reality is that no one has the power to make you happy; you need to do it yourself.

The problem for the governments around the world is that we tend to compare ourselves with others to gain perspective in our lives. Therefore, when my mum and dad purchased their first colour television in the mid-1960s they were overjoyed because most people in our road didn't have a TV. However, today because of the instant media coverage of everything, especially anything 'celebrity', we tend to compare ourselves with filthy rich footballers who we hear have their own Dolby surround-sound mini-cinemas. The grass really isn't greener on the other side.

Apparently advertising makes us less happy as it teases us with what we don't have and that which others do. We are shown images of other people (actors of course), who have a whole range of things in their life, that we should have and these 'have-it-alls' are patently very happy; and thus we are suitably unhappy until we buy their products! The Himalayan Kingdom of Bhutan makes policy based upon the Gross National Happiness and as a result it bans street advertising, MTV, plastic bags and wrestling on TV. As an aside it is worth noting that the Kingdom of Bhutan is not currently a democracy, although does this mean that the real answer to happiness is as simple as a WWF (World Wrestling Federation)-free world?

On recent surveys of happiness, Switzerland came first with the happiest citizens and in the UK we came eighth. A study by a team from the universities of Sheffield and Manchester, using data from the British Household Panel Survey, found that the happiest place in Britain was the sparsely populated Welsh county of Powys. Before you jump to the obvious conclusion that it's all that space and quiet time that is behind this, think again. The second happiest place in Britain is that wet, sprawling metropolis of Manchester. Even more surprising is that Edinburgh, without doubt one of the world's most beautiful cities, was found to be the most miserable place in Britain. Some people are never happy.

According to the BBC, 81 per cent of us have happiness as a goal compared to greater wealth at only 13 per cent. Bizarrely, when asked if we would want a drug that induced happiness and had no side-effects, 72 per cent of people said 'no' and only 26 per cent said 'yes'. Clearly we don't want an artificial life but a real life, with all its ups and downs. Don't you find this hugely inspiring and reassuring?

One of the biggest problems with having too high an expectation of happiness is that one can't control the uncontrollable and events happen that are beyond our control. After the tragic loss of a spouse it can take years to regain our previous state of well-being. Without good health, life is very challenging and even events such as divorce or losing a job can affect people's self-confidence for years. Psychologists tell us that our ability to be happy is determined by two things – our genes and our circumstances. We can't do anything about our genes, so we might as well accept this and move on.

Our life is affected by, first, our life circumstances and, second, our behaviour and activity. However, the good news is we can influence this and psychologists suggest this influence or leverage can be between 10 per cent and 15 per cent, although I suspect it is much greater than this. Our self-identity is a key factor in determining the life we lead, which is why so many lottery winners find life challenging once, by chance, great wealth attaches itself to them.

We can shift our self-identity but it isn't easy, and usually this only happens when we feel an urgent need to avoid emotional pain in our life or after a life-changing event. However, we do need change to stay happy and psychologists refer to hedonic adaptation, which, although it sounds like a strange sexual offshoot of witchcraft, is in fact the effect of getting bored and thus having reduced derived pleasure from repeated exposure to the same activities.

One heart-warming fact is that friends and loved ones are essential to a happy life and Professor Oswald of Warwick University estimates that a good friend is worth £50,000, as you need at least this to make up for the lost value in your life of losing a good friend. These scientists are all heart, aren't they? This is why our spouse, parents and children are irreplaceable – oops, nearly forgot; and siblings!

A team from the University College London found that those people who were less happy had higher levels of a bloodstream chemical called plasma fibrinogen, which is one of the indicators of the risk of developing heart disease in the future. This was one of the first pieces of research to confirm that happiness is chemically linked to a healthy heart. We all know unhappiness adversely affects our health through the negative impact of stress and pressure, but now we can rest assured that 'a happy heart is a healthy heart'.

A survey of nuns who attended the Sisters of Notre Dame, Milwaukee since 1930 found that happy nuns lived nine years longer than unhappy nuns. Clearly all other factors and life circumstances in the convent would be virtually the same for each nun and therefore this is a very interesting finding. We could summarise the findings in the style of our sensationalist media: 'Happy people who don't watch TV or have sex, on average, live nine years longer.'

Scientists say that on average smoking a packet of cigarettes a day reduces one's life expectancy by three years and therefore being happy is a big deal in terms of one's health. Of course, if you don't smoke and are also happy you possibly add 12 years to your life.

The flipside of peaceful happiness is that of anger, and my general impression is that life is getting more and more stressful and we seem to be seeing increasingly angry behaviour among our fellow citizens. This seems to be confirmed by a report from Dr Andrew McCulloch of the Mental Health Foundation. The study suggests that people are getting angrier, with almost one in three of us having a close friend or family member who has trouble controlling their temper. One in five people ended relationships with people because of how they behaved when they were angry. Anger can affect a range of physiological aspects – fatigue, sleep dysfunction, addiction, weight gains, lowered sex drive and loneliness – none of which are good things. Anger elevates cortisol levels in the body which causes a slower metabolism, and thus you put on weight and last longer when downed in the English Channel.

The psychologists say that you can't make a grumpy person into a happy person, although everyone can make changes. I like to believe that we can all make significant changes to our behaviour, even though we have to accept our genetic make-up. Therefore, rather than judge people, let's take a look at some of the behaviours that any of us might inadvertently fall into and which create quite a number of life's frustrations, all delivered by our fellow citizens.

The most common of these behaviours is 'yes-but'. This is when you say something that you feel is insightful and helpful and their response starts with 'yes-but', which basically means 'no'. Next on the list is 'it's not fair', which is the underpinning belief that drives virtually every one of their conversations. 'It's not fair I got a speeding fine (even though I was driving at 39 mph in a 30-mph zone and regularly do so)' or 'It's not fair that people have more money than me (even though they work harder than me and take more risks)'.

Next up is 'the problem is' which involves focusing upon a

negative imperfection in every one of life's experiences. 'The problem is, it's all very well being honest but what's the point when no one else is?' or, 'The problem is it's hardly perfect, is it?' This is what this behaviour feeds on, lack of perfection, because perfection is impossible to achieve and that's the problem.

Next up is the habitual interrupter, the 'I know, but', who will never let you actually finish any more than a couple of sentences without jumping in and interrupting you. This behaviour prohibits them from listening to what you are actually saying and you have a feeling they have their next sentence ready in their head before you even finish yours. Finally, the 'me-me' behaviour that involves an almost childlike need to be the centre of attention and which views the world only through that person's own eyes. Conversations will always be brought back to their experiences and you have the feeling that they have no interest whatsoever in you or your own experiences, thoughts and beliefs. Of course, all this is driven by insecurity as are so many of the less-than-attractive behaviours we all occasionally participate in. We all do this type of thing (except me and you, of course), and therefore the only solution is to laugh at our funny ways.

Scientists are now increasingly clear that people's attitudes to life have a direct bearing upon their health and therefore how we feel, think and thus behave does matter. Dr Hilary Tindle and her team at the University of Pittsburgh studied nearly 100,000 women and found that optimistic women had a 9 per cent lower risk of developing heart disease and a 14 per cent lower risk of dying. Women who harboured hostile or cynical thoughts were found to be 16 per cent more likely to die over the eight-year period of the study. These staggering findings confirmed earlier work on men's health by a Dutch team of scientists. US researchers as part of a ten-year study of 1,700 people published in the *European Heart Journal* in 2010 found that for each rise in their happiness scale there was a 22 per cent lower risk of developing heart disease. Therefore, it is apparently scientifically clear that a positive attitude to life, which must include smiling and laughing, often through life's inevitable adversities, is good for you and as Del Boy would say, 'You know it makes sense.'

Our journey through life's more amusing and interesting areas is almost at an end and we have focused upon some of the more bizarre aspects of British life and generally amusing behaviours the world over. We still do fairly well in this green and pleasant land of ours, certainly in comparison to many other countries. In our case the grass really isn't greener on the other side – well, maybe in New Zealand, but I doubt it. Our climate is moderate, our land always has a lush green hue and we rarely have to endure such extreme weather as tornados or hurricanes.

Whether you are born into an inner-city council estate or a country mansion, you can still have access to a minimum of 11 years of free education. We healthily mock political correctness rather than obey it and we still live in a free country where the media can hold our politicians to account and you can stand up on a soapbox in Hyde Park's Speakers' Corner and say virtually whatever you want, unless of course you are Jeremy Clarkson talking about Gordon Brown.

Our society and culture is fairly grown up, discerning and self-effacing. We innovate better than most other countries and our reality TV franchises rule the world. Free health care is still available to all (if you don't mind waiting) and we have one of the lowest murder rates in the world, although, one has to admit, we don't do so well with serial killers!

There are few better experiences than sitting in a cosy pub with friends or family, sipping ale or wine and feasting upon a ploughman's lunch with apple, pickled onions, a lump of Cheddar cheese and home-made crusty bread. When the sun shines in summer there really isn't any better place to be than Britain and on a frosty December night what could be better than to return home to your well-lit and warm house to snuggle up in front of the TV to watch some high-quality British drama? Then there is the wonderful aroma on Sunday of those traditional Sunday roasts cooking away in each household. We mustn't forget toad-in-the-hole, Marmite, a cup of tea, Scotch eggs, steak-and-kidney pie, chutney, marmalade, shepherd's pie, stew and dumplings, egg and chips, spotted dick (I'm ignoring political correctness here) and, of course, another nice cup of tea.

All this means you can sleep tight tonight knowing you live in the world's original democracy and I for one am very proud of this. I have said it before, and I make no apologies for saying it again; 'This is still a great place in which to live.' It is land where the vast majority of people are civilised, well-educated, reasonable and honest, so no wonder we like it here.

We started this book with our strange fascination with the weather and we have finished, as all things should, with a smile. Thank you for exploring life's funny side with me, thank you for hanging in there for a smile, and thank you for chuckling yourself. Because, as we know, 'Aren't we are a funny lot?'